T0077923

UNSPOKEN THOUGHTS

of Identical Twins

LYDELL *and* **LAYCELLE KING**

authorHOUSE

AuthorHouse™
1663 Liberty Drive
Bloomington, IN 47403
www.authorhouse.com
Phone: 833-262-8899

Published by AuthorHouse 06/02/2022

ISBN: 978-1-6655-6111-2 (sc)
ISBN: 978-1-6655-6112-9 (e)

Library of Congress Control Number: 2022910197

Print information available on the last page.

This book is printed on acid-free paper.

PREFACE

THESE ARE THE WORDS WHICH FORM MANY UNSPOKEN POEMS WRITTEN BY ME LAYCELLE KING AND MY IDENTICAL TWIN BROTHER LYDELL KING. AS YOU READ THROUGH OUR POEMS, MY BROTHER AND I TAKE YOU THE READER ON A JOURNEY OF MANY PAINFUL, LONELY, UNCERTAIN, FRIGHTENING AND FOREVER LOST DAYS AND NOW 23 YEARS OF OUR INCARCERATION. BEING INCARCERATED SINCE WE WHERE 15 YEARS YOUNG. MANY OF THESE POEMS EXPRESS OUR STRUGGLE FOR CHANGE, AND THE EMOTIONAL HUDDLES THAT WE NOT ONLY WENT THROUGH, BUT HAD TO LEARN TO DEAL WITH IN THE FACE OF STILL TRYING TO FIGURE OUT WHO WE WERE AND WHAT OUR PURPOSE IS ON THIS EARTH. AS WE GREW INTO MEN, IN A PLACE FILLED WITH SO MUCH NEGATIVITY, VIOLENCE. WE REALIZE ONE THING THAT NO ONE COULD NOT TAKE AWAY FROM US AND THAT WAS OUR UNSPOKEN WORDS. WHICH FORM MANY OF THESE POEMS.

ACKNOWLEDGEMENTS

MY BROTHER AND I WISH TO THANK THE MULTITUDE OF PEOPLE WHO HELPED, INSPIRED US TO WRITE THESE POEMS. THESE PEOPLE KNOW WHO THEY ARE. THANK YOU SHANNON KING, MY BEAUTIFUL WIFE FOR GIVING ME THE DRIVE TO CONTINUE TO WRITE. THANK YOU MOM FOR THE NEVER ENDING LOVE THAT YOU SHOW US. THANK YOU TO OUR UTILE BROTHER ANSON YOU HAVE HELPED MAKE ALL THIS HAPPEN, AND ALL OUR FRIENDS THAT CONTINUE TO SUPPORT US, NOTHING BUT REAL LOVE YOUR WAY. MAY THESE WORDS TOUCH YOU SOME WAY, SOME HOW.

LYDELL & LAYCELLE KING

"MY GREATEST FEAR"

BY:

LYDELL & LAYCELLE KING

A SIGH IN THE DARKNESS, THE BREATH UPON MY NECK UNNERVING CHILL UPON MY SPINE, MY NERVES BECOME A WRECK, QUICKENING PACE AND QUICKER STILL, MY STRIDE I DO INCREASE, ESCAPE THE MADNESS OF THE DARK, TO BRING MY HEART AT EASE. CRAWLING SKIN AND DEEPENING DREAD, I DARE NOT TURN TO SEE CREEPING, DEATH A PALE WHITE HORSE, NOW CHARGING AFTER ME THROUGH THE CAUSE WAYS OF MY MIND. HE'S GAINING ON ME STILL PRAY THAT HE WILL CEASE THE CHASE, BUT KNOW HE WILL PIERCING SOUNDS OF METAL BLADES, MERE INCHES FROM MY HEAD, STILL WON'T TURN TO FACE MY FOE, YET I KNOW THAT HE IS THERE, SWEAT IS PORING DOWN MY FACE, THE STINGING IN MY EYES EXHAUSTING STARTS TO RUN IT'S COURSE. CUT INTO MY THIGHS, PAIN UNKNOWN RIPS THROUGH MY SOUL, FEAR OVER POWERS MY MIND AS I TURN TO GAZE AT DEATH, AMAZED AT WHAT I FIND, A MIRROR HANGING FROM NOWHERE,

GIANT REFLECTION I NOW SEE PEERING BACK INTO THE GLASS, MY GREATEST FEAR WAS ME. OFTEN TIMES OUR ENEMY IS FEAR, MORE FREQUENTLY THAT FEAR IS THE TRUTH ABOUT WHO WE REALLY ARE.

"THE THICKNESS WITHIN MY MIND"

BY

LYDELL KING

I LIVE IN A DARK FORBIDDEN PLACE IN MY MIND.
THE LIGHT IS DIM AND THE HAZE IS THICK.
SHADOWS ARE EVERYWHERE. THE TERRAIN IS
ROCKY AND UNSURE. MOVING AROUND IS DANGEROUS
HOW EVER IT IS NECESSARY TO AVOID THE HAZE
AND THE SLUDGE OF THE SHADOWS. I SURVIVE ON
DREAMS OF PROMISING LIGHT AND SALVATION.
THEY BRING HOPE, BUT THEY MAY JUST BE A CURSE
TO PROLONG THE AGONY.
I LIVE ALONE WITH THE WIND BLOWING HATEFUL
WHISPERS AT MY THOUGHTS. FEAR STRANGLES
ME BECAUSE I AM CONNECTED TO THE HAZE LIKE
A SIAMESE TWIN.

"FRAGMENTS"

BY:
LAYCELLE KING

FRAGMENTS OF YOUR IMAGE I'LL FOREVER HOLD
FOR YOU ARE MY BEAUTIFUL QUEEN
AND THAT SOON TO BE TOLD.
I'M TRYING TO CLUTCH WITH MY MIND WHAT MY BODY
CAN'T TOUCH, AND THAT IN IT SELF IS NOT ENOUGH..
MY LIFE IS FULL OF WORDS AND MY WORDS ARE FULL OF
LIFE, NOW WITH YOU I CAN'T BEGIN TO GIVE UP A FIGHT OR
BEGIN MY JOURNEY THROUGH THIS LIFE LONG NIGHT WHICH
SURROUNDS ME, A NIGHT WHICH HOLDS ME IN IT'S GRASP..
WITH YOUR HEART IT WILL BRING A LIGHT WHICH IS SURE TO
GLEAM LIKE A SPARKLE OF A STAR HIDDEN IN THE SKY..
THESE WORDS I SPEAK ARE THE WORDS I REAP,
AND THIS I NOT CHEEP...

"SENTIMENT OF MY FLESH"

BY:
LYDELL KING

AS I LOOK UPON YOUR PICTURES, I SEE SENTIMENTS
OF MY FLESH. FOR YOU ARE MY DAUGHTER AND I
I'M HAPPY AS CAN BE.
DADDY IS PROUD OF YOU IN MORE WAYS THEN ONE,
YOU HAVE CONTINUED TO STAY STRONG, FOR
YOU ARE THE SENTIMENT OF MY FLESH.
I HAVE WATCHED YOU GROW BEFORE MY EYES,
STRONG AND WISE THROUGH PICTURES AND LETTERS,
IT HURTS ME SO INSIDE THAT I CAN'T BE BY YOUR
SIDE, TO HELP YOU THROUGH THE LIES THAT THE
WORLD THROW BEFORE YOUR EYES, FOR YOU
ARE THE SENTIMENT OF MY FLESH.
I LOVE YOU LIKE NO OTHER LATISHA, MY DAUGHTER,
MY HEART, MY WORLD, FOR YOU ARE THE
SENTIMENT OF MY FLESH.

5

"TEARS"

◆◆◆◆◆

BY:
LAYCELLE KING

TEAR DROPS DROP FROM MY EYES
AND FILL THE PAGE..
THE PAGE WHICH HOLDS MY RAGE. I FEEL MY MIND
SCREAMING A THOUSAND TIMES
FASTER THEN YESTERDAY..
I'M BEING BAPTIZED FROM THE TEARS THAT'S
SLOWLY DROPPED FROM MY EYES..
LORD ONLY KNOWS I NEED TO BE SAVED INSTEAD
OF BEING THAT SLAVE
THAT'S LEAD OUT TO PASTER..
FOR YEARS NOW I'VE DUG MY OWN HOLES OF
PAIN AND BLAMED THEM ON OTHERS, LETTING
MY STUPIDITY CUT TO THE QUICK LIKE BUTTER,
I HOPE TO PUT AN END TO MY SINS AS I SLOWLY
WRITE THIS POEM DOWN WITH THIS PEN..
IF I COULD DIE A THOUSAND TIMES TO WASH ALL
MY SINS AWAY, I WOULD SO I CAN CRY ONLY ONCE.

"THE COLOR BLUE"

BY:
LYDELL KING

BLUE IS THE COLOR WHICH COVERS THE SKY, IT'S
ALSO THE BACKGROUND UP HIGH, WHERE BIRDS FLY.
BLUE IS RELAXING AND PRETTY IN MINDS, IT'S
ALSO THE COLOR OF TH TEARS WE CRY. BLUE WAS
MY BACK BONE BACK IN THE DAY, IT'S ALSO MY
THOUGHTS AT NIGHT WHEN I PRAY.
BLUE IS THE COLOR OF THE DEEP BLUE SEA, IT'S
A PLACE I DREAM AND WISH TO BE.
BLUE IS THE COLOR WHICH REPRESENTS YOU,
BLUE IS OUR LOVE, AND FRIENDSHIP THROUGH AND
THROUGH...

"ROSES"

BY:
LAYCELLE KING

MANY DIFFERENT COLORS THAT MEAN DIFFERENT
THINGS, IT'S ALWAYS NICE TO SEE THE JOY
THAT ROSES BRING. OCCASIONS GOOD OR
OCCASION BAD, OCCASIONS HAPPY AND OCCASION SAD.

IT'S NEVER WRONG TO GIVE A ROSE, NOW
THAT'S JUST SOME THING THAT A TRUE FRIEND KNOWS..
ENCLOSED ARE SOME PEDALS YOU SHOULD
THROW THEM ON THE GROUND, THEY SHOULD
ALWAYS BE THERE WHEN A QUEEN WALKS AROUND.
IN MY EYES YOU ARE LOVELY, THE ONLY QUEEN BEE,

AND THAT SHOULD BE PLAIN FOR EVERY MAN
TO SEE.. NOW MOST ARE BLIND TO LIFES
WONDERFUL THINGS.. SO THANKS ONCE AGAIN
FOR THE JOY YOUR LOVE AND FRIENDSHIP BRING.

"TOO LONG"

BY:
LYDELL KING

IT HAS BEEN TOO LONG SINCE MY WORDS PAST
YOUR EYES AND GAVE YOU THAT HIDDEN SURPRISE
THAT LIGHTS UP YOUR EYES LIKE THE 4TH OF JULY.

IT HAS BEEN TOO LONG SINCE I HAVE LAID MY
EYES ON SUCH A BEAUTIFUL QUEEN, OH WHAT IT
MEANS TO ME TO BE REMINDED THAT I AM A KING
AND YOU ARE TRULY MY QUEEN. WHICH DRIVES
THIS MACHINE, WHICH MOST CALL A MAN.

AS IT CONTINUES TO BE TOO LONG, VISIONS
OF YOU IS ALL I SEE AND WHAT WE CAN BE, I
UNDERSTAND THAT YOU HAVE BEEN HURT
AND DON'T TRUST EASILY,
YET BABY IT HAS BEEN TOO LONG,
SO BABY OPEN UP YOUR HEART AND SEE WHAT CAN BE.

STATEMENT OF LOVE-

◆·◆·◆·◆·◆·◆·◆

BY: LAYCELLE KING

MY LOVE FOR YOU BEGAN THE DAY I TOLD YOU
THE TRUTH ABOUT MY SITUATION. MY LOVE FOR
YOU MANIFESTED ITSELF THROUGHOUT THE DAYS,
MONTHS AND NOW YEARS...
I'VE SHEDDED SO MANY TEARS, BECAUSE THE FEAR
OF LOSING YOU KEEP SHOWING IT'S TERRIFYING
IMAGE BEFORE MY VERY EYES..
I AM THE BLOOD IN YOUR BODY WHICH IS RED,
YOUR VEINS WHICH IS GREEN, AND YOUR BEAUTIFUL
SKIN WHICH IS A SO BEAUTIFUL CARMAL COLOR.
OUR SOULS ARE BOUND FOR THE SAME
DESTINATION, WHICH IS TRUE HAPPINESS,
BETWEEN ONE ANOTHER. FOR OUR STRUGGLE IN
THE PAST I GIVE YOU MY LOVE, LOYALTY, TRUST
AND MOST OF ALL HONESTY, THIS IS MY
STATEMENT OF LOVE TO YOU..

"THE MOUTH OF THE DEVILS DEN"

‹ ‹ ◆ ‹ ‹ ◆ ‹ ‹

BY:

LYDELL KING

THE MONTH OF THE DEVILS DEN RUNS THIN
WHEN IT HAS A BLACK KING IN IT TO WIN.
FOR THE WORLD WE LIVE IN IS A CONTINUING
SIN WERE MOST DON'T WIN, THOSE THAT DO,
HAVE TO DEFEND WHATS RIEFFLY NOT THEIRS.
FOR THIS WORLD WAS BUILT ON THE BLOOD AND
TEARS OF THE GODS AND GODDESSES THAT'S ABOVE THEM.
YET THE MOUTH OF THE DEVILS DEN AND THOSE
THAT FIND THEMSELVES IN IT, CONTINUE TO TRY TO IMPREGNATE
MINDS OF OUR FUTURE KINGS AND
QUEEN WITH THOUGHTS THAT
WILL ONLY LEAD TO THEIR EARLY DEPARTER FROM THIS EARTH.
WE CAN NOT CONTINUE TO REVAL IN THE PAST,
TRUE GODS AND GODDESSES ARE
DIVINE ORIGINS AND THE SOONER WE WILL BE
FREE FROM THE MOUTH OF THE DEVILS DEN..

FLOWERS

✦ ✦ ✦ ✦ ✦ ✦ ✦

BY: LAYCELLE KING

WALKING IN A FIELD OF FLOWERS
SIDE BY SIDE WITH YOU.
YOUR KISS IS REFRESHING LIKE AN APRIL SHOWER,
HOWEVER I PLAYED THE FOOL.
JUST LIKE THE WINTER WEATHERS THE ROSE,
TIME PASSED BY, OUR LOVE GREW COLD.
YOU TOLD ME IN LETTERS, TIME AND TIME
AGAIN, OUR LOVE WAS FOREVER, WE'D NEVER
END. NOW I SAW IT COMING, I KNEW FROM
THE START, ONE DAY LADY, WE'D FALL APART,
I SIT ALONE THINKING HOW TO MAKE IT RIGHT
I'D PLAYED THE FOOL AGAIN, IF ONLY FOR ONE NIGHT..
IF I EVER GET A CHANCE TO PROVE
MY LOVE MY LADY I'LL FOREVER WALK IN THOSE
FLOWERS SIDE BY SIDE WITH YOU..

YOU MAKE ME A BETTER MAN-

BY:
LYDELL KING

EVERY SINCE THE FIRST DAY I LAVED EYES
ON YOU, YOU MADE ME WANT TO BE A BETTER MAN.
I LOOKED INTO YOUR SO SUPPLICANT EYES,
FOR THEY DON'T TELL NO LIES, FOR THEY ARE
THE WINDOWS TO THE SOUL, AS I CONTINUED
TO CONNECT WITH YOU, FROM ONE LOOK, I
KNEW RIGHT THEN AND THERE THAT YOU WOULD
MAKE ME A BETTER MAN.
NOT IN A THOUSAND YEARS WOULD I HAVE THOUGHT
THAT I WOULD BE HAPPY FOR FOUR STRAIGHT YEARS,
YOU MAKE ME A BETTER MAN.
I'VE SHUT OUT ALL THE TALES ABOUT HOW WE
WOULD NOT MAKE IT, HOW YOU WOULD FALTER
AND GO ASTRAY, YET I HAVE KEPT HOPE ALIVE,
FOR I TRULY UNDERSTAND THAT YOU ARE THAT
SPECIAL WOMAN THAT HAS MAD ME INTO A
MUCH BETTER MAN.

MISSING YOU-

BY: LAYCELLE KING

I MISS THE TIMES WE USED TO SHARE,
MY LOVE WAS ALL I HAD TO SPARE,
I HAD THIS FEELING DEEP IN MY MIND
THAT WE COULD STAY TOGETHER TILL
THE END OF TIME...
I THINK IN THE DAY AND DREAM AT NIGHT,
THAT ONE DAY THE LOVE WE SHARED WILL
REUNITE...
MAYBE IT WILL AND MAYBE IT WON'T, LIFE
GOES ON AND WE WILL BOTH KNOW, THERES
A PLACE IN MY HEART THAT'S WARM AND TRUE,
IF YOU EVER NEED SOMEONE
TO COMFORT YOU, REMEMBER
THAT PLACE THAT'S OPEN ONLY TO YOU...

THE DEPTH OF TIME-

BY:
LYDELL KING

THE DEPTH OF TIME IS HARD FOR SOME TO GRASP
AT TIMES, YET IT'S THIS DEPTH THAT KEEPS
HOPE ALIVE AND MOST LOOKING TOWARD THE
FUTURE AND WHAT TH FUTURE HOLDS.
IT IS THIS DEPTH THAT HELPS ME MANIFEST

MY FEELINGS ABOUT YOU AND I AND WHERE
WE SHOULD TRULY BE.
IT IS YOU THAT I WANT TO SHARE THIS DEPTH
WITH MY QUEEN, YOU ARE THE ONE THAT I SEE

IN MY DREAMS AT NIGHT, IT IS YOU THAT I
SEE IN THE DEPTH OF MY SOUL AS WELL AS THE
DEPTH OF MY TIME.

FIRST LETTER-

BY:
LAYCELLE KING

WHEN WE FIRST WROTE, I KNEW THAT IT
WAS MORE THEN A NOTE..

OR THAT'S WHAT I HOPED.
WELL I HAVE TO HOPE NO MORE,
BECAUSE YOU BROUGHT LIGHT TO MY SHORE
WHICH WAS SO DARK AND SO LONELY,
YOU WERE THE ONLY ONE THAT I TRULY
TRUSTED AND THE ONE THAT I
TRULY LUSTED FOR..
I RUMMAGED THROUGH MY MIND AND THINK,
IF WE WERE ONE, YOU AND I TOGETHER
WOULD MAKE A UNIVERSE THAT COULD SHAKE
THE STARS, AND MOVE THE HEAVENS.

"CRASHING IN"

BY:
LYDELL KING

THINGS ARE CRASHING IN WITHIN MY OWN
SOUL AS I MANIFEST AND RECONCESS
MY FEELINGS OF THE WORLD THAT I NOW
FIND MYSELF IN.
IN A WORLD OF HATRED AND BIGOTRY
A YOUNG BLACK MAN DWELLS, FOR I UNDERSTAND
THAT I AM HATED FOR WHO I HAVE BECOME
AND NOT FOR WHO THEY WANTED ME TO BE
THE GAME THAT TWISTS PEOPLES MINDS
AND CHANGE THEIR THOUGHTS ALWAYS
SEEM TO EMERGE AT THE MOST
STENOUSE TIMES.
YET I RELINQUISH MY PAST THAT HAUNTS MY FUTURE
WHICH HAS PUSHED ME INTO
THE MAN I AM TODAY, THERE FOR
THERE IS NO MORE CRASHING IN.

"WORDS"

BY:
LAYCELLE KING

I WRITE THESE WORDS IN PLACE OF MY TEARS.
THE WORDS FLOW, FLOODING THE PAPER, LIKE
DROPS OF RAIN HEALING THE EARTH, HEALING
MY HEART, HEALING MY SPIRIT..
NEVER ENDING PAIN NOURISHING BY NEVER
ENDING WORDS..
AS I WRITE THESE WORDS, THE CHANGES
INSIDE BECOME CLEARER AS I WRITE THESE
MY PHYSICAL IS LOCKED DOWN, HOWEVER MY MIND IS FREE..
AS I WRITE THESE WORDS THE WORLD
CONTINUES TO SPIN..
AS I WRITE THESE WORDS THE FACE OF THIS
PAGE CHANGES BECOMING A MESSAGE..
WHAT BEAUTY OF WORDS.

CRIES WITHIN MY SOUL-

BY:
LYDELL KING

CRIES WITHIN MY SOUL IS WHAT
THE REAPER TOLD ME, WHEN HE
IMPREGNATED THE JUDGES HEART
AND MIND TO TRY AND END TWO
BLACK MINDS.
YET WHAT THE REAPER DID NOT KNOW,
THESE CRIES WITHIN MY SOUL HAS ME
FEELING REAL BOLD, FOR I WAS TOLD
AND NOW I TRULY UNDERSTAND THAT
I AM A MAN.
A MAN THAT'S DESTINE TO BE THE TRUE KING
THAT GOD WANTED ME TO BE.

I ENDED MY LIFE BEFORE I STARTED MY LIFE-

BY:

LAYCELLE KING

I WAS YOUNG, I WAS DUMB, ALWAYS LOOKING FOR
THE THINGS THAT NEVER CAME.
ALWAYS TRYING TO CLAIM THE FAME, WHEN I
REALLY DIDN'T KNOW THE MEANING OF MY NAME.
IT'S A SHAME TRYING TO CLAIM THE FAME
AND NOT KNOW YOUR NAME.
I WAS A FOOL TRYING TO FIT IN. MY MOM
SHOWED ME LOVE, SHOWED ME HOW TO CARE HOW
EVER I TOOK THAT AND PUT IT IN THE AIR LIKE I DIDN'T CARE.
AND NOW AS YOU CAN TELL I'M IN HELL. TRYING
NOT TO DWELL ON THE THINGS I HAD AND THE
THINGS THAT I SHOULD HAVE HAD.
PEOPLE SAY LEAVE ALL THE PAST BEHIND AND START
A NEW LIFE, HOWEVER HOW CAN I START
A NEW LIFE WHEN I REALLY DIDN'T HAVE A LIFE AT THE AGE OF 15.
I SHOULD HAVE LISTENED TO MY MOM FROM THE START THEN
I KNOW WE WOULD NOT BE APART. HOWEVER I HAD TO GO
MY OWN WAY AND I DID, AND NOW I'M PAYING FOR IT AT
THE AGE OF 17 WHEN MY LIFE JUST STARTED.

(CONCRETE HELL)

BY:
LYDELL KING

I SIT IN MY CAGE AND
WHAT DO I SEE? CONFUSION,
HATRED AND DISLIKE ALL AROUND ME.
I TRY TO BLOCK IT OUT,
THE PAIN SEEM TO COME
EARTH DAY, NO MATTER
HOW HARD I TRY IT WON'T GO AWAY.
IN A PLACE WITH STILL
WALLS, AND LONG TIERS,
PEOPLE SIT RESTLESSLY
THE COMING YEARS.
LIFE ISN'T FAIR AND THIS I KNOW,
HOWEVER I TRY TO KEEP A SMILE
AND GO WITH THE FLOW OF LIFE.
SOME TIMES LUCK FALLS IN MY LAP,
MOST OF THE TIME
I CRAP OUT, HOWEVER THAT'S
JUST SOMETHING, THIS LIFE IS ABOUT.

UPON AWAKING-

BY:

LAYCELLE KING

I AM CAUGHT IN AN ILLUSION WITHIN THE MIX
OF CONFUSION OF THIS PRISON LIFE. WHICH
BIGHTS AT MY FORBIDDEN SOUL WHICH HAS
AHOLD OF MY VERY SENCITIVE FRONTAL LOMB.
I'VE BEEN TOLD, THE ONE WHO HOLD THE KEY TO
HIS OWN HEART CAN BEGIN TO STAND ON HIS
OWN IN THIS VERY IMPERSONAL WORLD.
IN THIS SETTING I AM BETING THAT GREAT
MINDS ARE GOING TO WAIST, AND ARE LOST
IN TIME LIKE THE ANCIENT SHRINES.
MY BRAINS LIKE A KNIFE, I CUT THROUGH LIFE.
I CUT TO THE CHASE OF THIS MENTAL DASE,
A DASE THAT DON'T HAVE NO FACE.
A BASE THAT OFTEN FINDS MOST PEOPLE
REALITY WHICH MOST OFTEN ENDS IN A
FATALITY. AS I
WALK THIS LOST SOUL PRISON YARD, I SEE MANY PEOPLE
PULLING EATH OTHERS CARDS, TRYING TO FIGURE THEY REALLY
ARE AMONG THESE PRISON GUARDS WHO DON'T KNOW
WHO THEY ARE. MANY ARE SCARED AND
IN THAT ARE HIDDEN AFAR
AMONG THE LOST SOUL PRISON YARD.

THE SECRETES OF MY AFFECTION-

BY:

LYDELL KING

THE SECRETES OF MY AFFECTION, I SAW YOU FROM AFAR,
THE BEAUTY OF YOU JUST RADIATING OFF YOUR BODY,
SENDING UNCONTROLLABLE FEELINGS THROUGH
OUT MY BODY, RIGHT THEN AND THERE I KNEW THAT
YOU WAS THE SECRETES OF MY AFFECTION.

VISIONS OF YOU THROUGH OUT MY DREAMS, I
CONTINUE TO TELL MYSELF, I WON'T DECAY OR
FUALTER MY THOUGHTS, FOR IT'S YOU THAT'S
THE SECRETES OF MY AFFECTION.

I'VE VISIONED THIS MOMENT, DREAMED OF THIS
MOMENT, SECRETLY PLAYED OUT THIS MOMENT IN
MY MENTAL, I'VE LOVED YOU BEFORE I SET EYES ON
YOU, YOU ARE THE SECRETES OF MY AFFECTION.

AS I SIT HERE AND WATCH MY DREAMS TURN INTO
REALITY AND PUSH ALL MY PASSED CASUALTY$ TO
THE BACK OF ME, I FIND MYSELF FACED BEFORE YOU,
FOR YOU ARE THE SECRETES OF MY AFFECTION.

"APPEALS AND ORDEALS"

BY:

LAYCELLE KING

HOW DOUBTFUL IT DOES SEEM THAT HOPE
FOR MY APPEAL DOES NOT GLIME.
I WALK AROUND IN A DAZE. FOR ME NOT GETTING
ANY ACTION HAS ME GOING THROUGH A FAZE.
I WALK SIDE BY SIDE WITH MY SOUL AND HE HASN'T BEGAN
TO TELL ME WHAT HAS NOT BEEN TOLD.. FOR HE KNOWS HOW
I FEEL ABOUT THESE MESSED UP NEVER ENDING APPEALS.

IT SEEM I KEEP MY HOPES AND DREAMS IN THESE
NEVER ENDING SKEEMS WHICH KEEP THE WHEEL
OF MY ORDEAL A THRILL IN MY OWN MINE..

AS I DEPEND ON MY PEN IN WHICH I GRIP WITH M RIGHT
HAND, I'M NEVER LOCKED IN. AS I PIMP UP ON THIS PEN, I
WRITE DOWN THE WORDS, THAT MANY MAY THINK ARE A SIN.

WHICH ARE MY TRUE THOUGHTS, THAT HAS THIS WORRIOR
GOING DOWN A PATH ONLY FEW HAVE WALKED.

SO AS I LOOK OVER AT MY SOUL ONCE AGAIN, I
FIND MYSELF FREE LIKE THE HIDDEN GEM OF THE
EAST. AND THAT'S NOT A MAN IN WHICH YOU
WOULD CALL WEAK. HOWEVER A MAN WHOM
HAS FINALLY FOUND PEASE.

THE SUN AMONGST MY CLOUDS-

BY:
LYDELL KING

THE SUN AMONGST MY CLOUDS WHICH HAS BLURRED
MY VISION, YET THE GIMMER OF THE SUN THAT I
DO SEE THROUGH THE CLOUDS GIVES ME
HOPE THAT THERE WILL BE A BETTER TOMORROW..

AS THE SUN CONTINUES TO RADIATE ALL IT'S ESSENCE
UPON THE CLOUDS, THEY START TO EVAPORATE
CREATING THE TRUE FULL PICTURE OF WHAT LIFE IS
REALLY ABOUT. THE SUN AMONGST MY CLOUDS.

AS THE SUN STARTS TO TOUCH MY FLESH I AM CREATED ANEW,
I NO LONGER SEE LIFE IN THE SAME EYE AS I DID ONCE BEFORE,
I TRULY UNDERSTAND THAT I AM ANEW IN A MUCH BETTER,
STRONGER FORM, ALL DO TO THE SUN AMONGST MY CLOUDS.

NOW THAT I CAN SEE, I AM FREE, FREE TO BE WHO I
AM DESTINED TO BE, WHICH IS A MAN WITH A PLAN TO
SUCCEED LIKE THOSE BEFORE ME AND THOSE AFTER.

YOU MOM ARE THE SUN THAT HAS CLEARED MY CLOUDS
AND CREATED ME ANEW, I AM THE TRUE REFLECTION
OF YOU, THE SUN AMONGST MY CLOUDS.

YOU'RE MY ISLAND OF PARADISE-

BY:
LYDELL KING

AS MY TURBULENT WATERS RAGE AND CRASH UPON
THE SHORES OF MY SOUL,
YOU'RE MY SOLID GROUND ON SHIFTING SANDS OF TIME,
AS EVERY SLAMMING DOOR VIBRATES MY MIND,
YOU'RE THE FIRE THAT WARMS MY HEART IN
THE COLD, DREARY HOURS, YOU'RE THE FRUIT THAT
REPLENISHES MY STRENGTH AS I DO BATTLE WITH
LONELINESS, YOU'RE THE VOICE I HEAR WHISPERING
ON THE WINDS TO GUIDE ME SO I DON'T BECOME
LOST. AS YOUR TOUCH IS MY REALITY, YOU'RE THE
SAND AND I AM THE SEA, AND THOUGH EBB
AND FLOW MAY DIFFER LIKE THE SAND AND THE SEA,
I AM OF YOU AND YOUR OF ME.

IT'S NOT ENOUGH-

BY:
LAYCELLE KING

IT'S NOT ENOUGH TO HAVE A DREAM, UNLESS YOUR
WILLING TO PURSUE IT.

IT'S NOT ENOUGH TO KNOW WHAT'S RIGHT UNLESS
YOU'RE STRONG ENOUGH TO DO IT.

IT'S NOT ENOUGH TO JOIN A CROWD TO BE
AKNOWLEDGED AND ACCEPTED.
YOU MUST BE TRUE TO IDEAS, EVEN IF
YOU'RE LEFT OUT AND REJECTED.

IT'S NOT ENOUGH TO KNOW THE TRUTH UNLESS
YOU ALSO LEARN TO LIVE WITH IT

IT'S NOT ENOUGH TO REACH FOR LOVE UNLESS YOU
CARE ENOUGH TO GIVE IT.

THE WAY WE WERE

BY:
LAYCELLE KING

THE WAY WE WERE YESTERDAY
IS GONE, FOREVER. AND THE
WAY WE ARE TODAY IS
CONSTANTLY CHANGING. YET,
WE SHED ONLY A FEW TEARS,
FOR WE HAVE FIXED OUR EYES
ON THE WAY WE WILL BE TOMORROW.

4 EVER IS NOT ENOUGH-

BY:
LYDELL KING

AS I WOKE TODAY, AS I DO EVERY DAY, MY FIRST
THOUGHTS IS OF YOU. MY WIFE KESHA T. KING.
MY HEART START TO RACE AND I FIND
MYSELF LIKE A UTILE KID AGAIN.
YOU ARE MY WIFE, MY EVERY
THING, WHY DO IT SEEM LIKE 4 EVER IS NOT ENOUGH.

MOST WILL DOUBT US AND THAT'S GOOD, BECAUSE
I KNOW AND FEEL THAT THE LOVE THAT WE SHARE
WILL GET US THROUGH, WE HAVE AND SHARE
SOMETHING THAT'S MORE SPECIAL THEN WE TRULY
KNOW, 4 EVER IS NOT ENOUGH.

PEOPLE HAVE DIED AND CREATED NEW LIFE, YET
THEY STILL DREAM TO HAVE WHAT WE SHARE, WE
HAVE HAD OUR TRIALS AND TRIBULATIONS TO GET
US READY FOR EACH OTHER, AND NOW THAT WE
HAVE EACH OTHER, IT SEEMS LIKE 4 EVER IS
NOT ENOUGH.

EVERYNIGHT-

BY:
LAYCELLE KING

EVERYNIGHT WHEN I THINK, I THINK
ABOUT YOU.
EVERYNIGHT WHEN I TALK,
I TALK ABOUT YOU.
EVERYNIGHT WHEN I WRITE,
I WRITE TO OR ABOUT YOU.
DO YOU SEE A PATTERN HERE?
I DO.
IT'S YOU!

OF KINGS AND QUEENS-

———— ✦✦✦✦✦ ————

BY:
LYDELL KING
&
KESHA KING

WE SHARE SOMETHING THAT MOST CAN ONLY DREAM
OF, YET" WE HAVE," YOU HAVE ALLOWED ME TO BE ME
AND YOU BE YOU, WE ARE OF KINGS AND QUEENS.

YOU KESHA HAVE BECOME MY STAR, MY LIGHT OF
HOPE, MY QUEEN THAT TRULLY UNDERSTANDS HER
KINGS STRUGGLE.

WE SHARE A BOND THAT MOST PEOPLE ONLY WISH
FOR, YET "WE ARE," YOU ARE MY SHINING,
STRONG KING AND I AM YOUR BEAUTIFUL BLAZING QUEEN.

YOU LYDELL HAVE BECOME MY ROCK, MY DEFENDER
AND PROTECTOR. MY KING WHO TRULY
UNDERSTANDS HIS QUEENS BROKEN AND BATTERED HEART.

SITUATIONS PAST AND PRESENT HAS PREPARED US FOR
ALL SITUATIONS, HAS PREPARED US FOR EACH OTHER,
AND THAT'S FOR LIFE AND JUST NOT FIVE MINUTES.

THE RISING OF THE SUN-

BY:

LAYCELLE KING

LAST NIGHT BY THE LIGHT OF THE MOON, WE
WALKED SIDE BY SIDE, HAND IN HAND ALONG
THE SANDY BEACH. WE SHARED OUR MEMORIES
OF THE PAST, AND WHAT ALL WE'VE BEEN THROUGH,
DURING THAT TIME,
WE WALKED, WE TALKED, WE LAUGHED, WE CRIED,
THEN YOU LAYED DOWN AND SOFTLY SANG ME TO SLEEP.
ALL NIGHT WE CARESSED ONE ANOTHER,
AND HELD EACH OTHER TIGHTLY,
NEVER WANTING TO LET GO.
THE NIGHT WAS MISTY AND COLD, BUT WENT UNNOTICED, AS
WE WERE WRAPPED UP IN THE HOT SWEET PASSION WE SHARED.
I WAKE UP TO THE RISING OF THE SUN, DISAPPOINTED, LOST
AND CONFUSED, FOR I AM NO LONGER IN YOUR ARMS.

I'M SITING HERE ALL ALONE, REPLAYING MY DREAM IN
MY MIND, TRYING TO DECIDE WHETHER OR NOT IT WAS
REAL, AND IF IT WAS, HOW COULD YOU BE GONE SO
FAST? I FINALLY FACE THE TRUTH, BUT KEEP FAITH IN MY
HEART, CAUSE I KNOW ONE MORNING, I WILL WAKE UP
TO THE RISING OF THE SUN, AND YOUR SWEET FACE.

GETTING THROUGH TOUGH TIMES-

BY:
LYDELL KING

FACING OUR DIFFICULT DAYS IS ONE OF THE HARDEST THINGS
ONE IS EVER ASKED TO DO. THERE ARE TIMES WHEN WE FEEL LIKE
OUR BLUE SKIES ARE TO FAR AWAY THEN THEY'VE EVER BEEN.
AND WE'D GIVE ANYTHING TO GET OUR SMILES BACK AGAIN.
IF THOSE KINDS OF FEELINGS EVER COME TO YOU AND I KNOW
THEY DO, MAYBE THESE WORDS HELP GET YOU THROUGH.

I'M SORRY TO KNOW THAT YOU'RE GOING THROUGH
A TOUGH TIME, I WOULD GIVE ANYTHING IF I COULD
JUST SNAP MY FINGERS AND EVERYTHING WOULD GET
RIGHT, LIFE DOESN'T ALWAYS PLAY BY THE RULES, THOSE
REMINDERS COME TO US ALL, IT DON'T MAKE THINGS
EASIER TO KNOW THAT THINGS ARE SO UNFAIR, YET I HOPE
IT DOES MAKE IT A UTILE BETTER TO KNOW THAT I CARE.

I WANT YOU TO REMEMBER THAT I AM ON YOUR TEAM
AND TIME IS TO. REASSURANCE AND HAPPINESS IS
WITH IN YOU, JUST WAITING TO BE REDISCOVERED,

BEFORE TO LONG YOUR DAYS WILL BE LEFT BEHIND AND YOUR
HEART WILL GUIDE YOU AS YOU GO ON EVERY STEP YOU
TAKE ON YOUR PATH. ALL YOUR INNER STRENGTH, ABILITY
AND WISDOM WILL WALK ALONG BESIDE YOU, HELPING
TO GUIDE YOU OVER ANY HARD SPOTS YOU TAKE.

THROUGH THESE TOUGH TIMES YOU WILL BE MAKING
GOOD TRANSITIONS EVERY STEP OF THE WAY. EVERY
DAY WILL GET EASIER AND AS YOU GO ALONG CLOSER
TO THEM SPECIAL SEASONS OF YOUR LIFE, I HOPE THAT
YOU WILL BE GIVEN EVERY REASON TO BELIEVE THAT.

WHAT EVER LIFE LACKS IN STOPPING OUR SORROW, IT MAKES
UP FOR WITH THOUSANDS OF BRIGHTER TOMORROWS

I KNOW MY SOUL-

BY:
LAYCELLE KING

I PLUCKED MY SOUL OUT OF IT'S SECRET PLACE,
AND HELD IT TO THE MIRROR OF MY EYE, TO
SEE IT LIKE A STAR AGAINST THE SKY. A

TWITCHING BODY QUIVERING IN SPACE,
A SPARK OF PASSION SHINING ON MY FACE.

I EXPLORED IT TO DETERMINE WHY THIS AWFUL
KEY TO MY INFINITY CONSPIRES TO ROB ME OF

SWEET JOY AND GRACE. IF THE SIGH MAY NOT
BE FULLY READ IF I CAN COMPREHEND, NOT

CONTROL, I NEED NOT GLOOM MY DAYS WITH FRUTILE DREAD,
BECAUSE I SEE A PART AND

NOT THE WHOLE. CONTEMPLATING THE STRANGE,
I'M COMFORTED BY THIS NARCOTIC THOUGHT,
I KNOW MY SOUL, NOW AINT THAT LOVE?

FIGURE IT OUT-

BY:

LYDELL KING

JUST YESTERDAY YOU SAID YOU REALLY LOVED ME. I'VE FIGURED OUT JUST HOW TRUE IT WAS, YOU SAID I MAKE YOU HAPPY AND I TOLD YOU I WAS TRULY IN LOVE. THROW EVERY ONE ELSE OUT THE PICTURE AND LETS SEE WHAT COMES NEXT. I'LL LEAVE MY HEART IN YOUR HANDS BECAUSE THERE IT IS SAFE AND AT REST.

MORE LOVE THAN I HAVE EVER KNOWN, NEVER LEAVE ME, I WILL COME STRAIGHT HOME. I LOVE YOU BABY, WITH OUT A DOUBT, HOW LONG DID IT TAKE YOU TO REALLY FIGURE IT OUT?

MY HEART BEATS FOR YOU EVERY DAY AND EVERY NIGHT, I KNOW WITH YOU BY MY SIDE, EVERY THING WILL BE ALRIGHT, YOU BRING OUT THE BEST IN ME AND MAKE MY DAYS BRIGHT. I'LL LOVE YOU FOR A LIFE TIME MY LOVE, MY LIFE, I WILL TRY TO BE MORE OPEN AS TIME GOES ON, YET YOU KNOW MY SITUATION AND PAIN, SO PLEASE HELP ME, I KNOW YOU WILL BE THERE WHEN EVER I NEED YOU TO. MY HAPPINESS, MY JOY, MY LOVE, THE WAY I LOOK AT LIFE, I OWE IT ALL TO YOU, WHY YOU LOVE ME SO MUCH, WHY YOU LOOK ME IN MY EYES THE WAY YOU DO? I DON'T KNOW YET, YET I'LL FIGURE IT OUT SOON.

"THE ACT OF ONES SELF"

BY:
LAYCELLE KING

WHO WOULD, WHO COULD UNDERSTAND THAT,
WHEN I HEAR YOU I AM A SKINNY, DUMB,
KNOCK KNEED DOG DROOLING ON THE WORDS
OF WHAT YOU SAY.
ME I'M A DOG NOT PANTING FOR A PAT
FROM YOUR HAND, SO I CAN WAG MY LOVE
IN FRONT OF YOUR FACE. A PRINCE HOPING WITH
LUST, WAITING FOR THE KISS OF ACTION FROM
MY PRINCESS. NOW I KNOW THAT THIS WHOLE

SCENE IS NOT COOL, BUT IT'S REAL. SOMETIMES
WE BE SO CLOSE I CAN FEEL YOUR PULSE AND

THINK IT'S MY HEART THAT I HEAR IN MY
EARS. NOW ANT THAT LOVE?

I'M READY-

◆◆◆◆◆◆

BY:
LYDELL KING

I'M READY FOR MORE THEN YOU EXPECT,
MY LOVE FOR YOU DOESN'T COUNT YET,
AFTER I GET TO WHERE YOU ARE, YOU
WILL SEE WHAT COMES NEXT, DON'T TAKE
THESE WORDS JUST AS A POEM I WROTE,
LOOK INTO MY HEART, THERE YOU WILL
SEE WHAT I'M READ FOR.
I'M READY, I'M READY FOR YOUR HEART
LIKE YOU ARE READY FOR MINE, I'M

READY TO COMMIT AND GIVE YOU ALL
MY TIME, MY HEART, MY SOUL, AND TRUE
LOVE DIVINE, ARE YOU FEELING MY WORDS?
ARE THEY REGISTERING IN YOUR MIND?
WILL YOU LOVE ME UNCONDITIONALLY?
ARE YOU READY FOR ME?
I'M MORE READY NOW THEN I WILL EVER
BE, SO I'M SAYING THIS TO SAY ONE TIME
AND ONE TIME ONLY, I'M READY.

MY ONE AND ONLY TRUE LOVE-

BY:
LAYCELLE KING

WHEN THE ROAD SEEMS TOO LONG WHEN THE
DARKNESS SETS IN, WHEN EVERYTHING TURNS OUT
WRONG AND YOU CAN'T SEEM TO FIND A
FRIEND, REMEMBER YOU ARE LOVED.

WHEN SMILES ARE HARD TO COME BY AND YOUR FEELING
DOWN, WHEN YOU SPREAD YOUR WINGS TO FLY AND YOU
CAN'T GET OFF THE GROUND, REMEMBER YOU ARE LOVED.

WHEN TIME RUNS OUT BEFORE YOU ARE THROUGH
AND IT'S OVER BEFORE YOU BEGIN, WHEN UTILE
THINGS START TO GET TO YOU AND IT FEELS LIKE YOU
JUST CAN'T WIN, REMEMBER YOU ARE LOVED.

WHEN YOUR LOVED ONCE ARE FAR AWAY AND YOU ARE ON
YOUR OWN, WHEN YOU DON'T KNOW WHAT TO SAY AND
YOU'RE AFRAID OF BEING ALONE, REMEMBER YOU ARE LOVED.

WHEN YOUR SADNESS COMES TO AN END AND EVERYTHING
GOES RIGHT, MAY YOU THINK OF YOUR FAMILY AND FRIENDS
AND KEEP THEIR LOVE INSIGHT, THANK YOU FOR BEING LOVED.

MAY YOU SEE THE LOVE AROUND YOU IN EVERY THING YOU DO,
AND WHEN TROUBLES SEEM TO SURROUND YOU, LET ALL MY
LOVE SHINE THROUGH, YOU ARE BLESSED, YOU ARE LOVED.

ENTRAPED-

BY:
LYDELL KING

ENTRAPPED IN THIS DARKNESS-
IS ALL I SEE, I SIT HERE AND
DWELL IN IT AND THINK TO MYSELF,
IS THIS HELL THAT HAS FOUND IT'S WAY
TO ENTRAP ME OR IS THIS MISERY AND
PAIN THAT WILL AND HAS MADE ME
STRONG AND INTO THE MAN I AM TODAY.
FOR THIS WORLD THAT I FIND MYSELF
SUBJECTED TO, ONLY BRAKES UP HAPPY
HOMES AND LOVED ONES, IT CAUSE
MISERY AND PAIN, FOR THIS WORLD
WAS MADE FOR ONLY THREE REASONS,
TO MAKE YOU OR BRAKE YOU AND CAUSE YOU
PAIN THE WHOLE STEP OF THE WAY.

"A SINGLE WISH"

BY:
LAYCELLE KING

I NEVER WAS MUCH OF A POET, AND NO GOOD
AT MAKING RHYMES, SO BARE WITH ME IF YOU
CAN, WHILE READING THESE FEW LINES.
IF I COULD MAKE A SINGLE WISH, AND KNOW

IT WOULD COME TRUE, THE ONLY THING THAT
I WOULD WISH IS TO BE WITH YOU.

I'D KISS YOUR LIPS AND SQUEEZE YOU TIGHT,
AND NEVER LET GO.

IN MY ARMS IS WHERE YOU WOULD BE,
IT'S ALL YOU WOULD KNOW.
I'D LAY YOU DOWN AGAINST MY FLESH,

AND MAKE LOVE TO YOU. THAT WOULD
BE THE BEST.

IF ONLY I COULD HAVE ONE WISH, THAT'S
WHAT I WOULD DO.

"LIKE NO OTHER"

BY:
LAYCELLE KING

I WANT YOU TO BE MY LOVER..
FOR WITH OUT YOU THERE WOULD BE
NO OTHER..
A LOVE LIKE YOURS, IS SO FEW, I
GUESS THAT'S WHY I LOVE YOU.
LOVING ME MAY NOT BE FUN,
HOWEVER IT'S WORTH IT ALL,
WHEN THIS TIME IS DONE..
SO HOLD ON BABY, AND SOON
YOU WILL SEE JUST HOW MUCH
YOU MEAN TO ME.
HEAVENLY FATHER UP ABOVE,
PLEASE PROTECT THE WOMAN
I LOVE, SHANNON KING.
IF SHE SHOULD DIE AND GO TO
HEAVEN, THEN IT WILL BE MY WISH
TO GO AS WELL.

"A MOTHERS WISH"

BY:
LAYCELLE KING

YOU HELD US IN YOUR WOMB NINE
MONTHS, BEFORE OUR LIFE...IN PAIN YOU GAVE US BIRTH, TWINS..
OUR FATHERS STRIFE, WE KNEW NOT WHO WE
WERE.. NO MEMORIES OF THAT TIME CAN BE
RECALLED THIS DAY, WITHIN OUR SEARCHING MINDS..
THE FIRST WORDS WE UTTERED WAS DAD OR
MOM.. IT SEEM SO LONG AGO..
A PRECIOUS TIME LONG GONE.. I'M
SURE OUR FIRST FEW STEPS, SO
SHORT AND SLOW OF PACE, LEFT PRINTS
UPON YOUR HEART, THAT
VERY SACRED PLACE... DID THEY BRING
YOU SORROW? FOR COMMON
SINCE DOES SAY I WASN'T MOVING TOWARD YOU.
IT MUST HAVE BEEN AWAY. AND AS I GREW
TO MAN HOOD, YOU TAUGHT ME MANY THINGS. I
MUST HAVE MISSED THE LESSONS OF SADNESS
LIFE CAN BRING. I'M WRITING TO YOU TODAY, I
THINK BACK TO THE TIMES YOU COULDN'T BE
PROUD OF ME.. FOR ALL MY SINFUL CRIMES. FOR I KNOW A

45

MOTHERS WISH, THOUGH NOT EXPRESSED ALOUD IS TO HAVE
LOVING SONS.. SONS TO MAKE YOU PROUD. IN LIFE COME FULL
CIRCLE. I'M ONCE AGAIN A CHILD, A CHILD BORN OF SPIRIT.
GOD FEARING, GENTLE, MILD, THE LESSONS THAT YOU
TAUGHT US, THEY'VE SERVED ME VERY WELL.
I STILL REMEMBER THE A, B, C's .. I USE THEM CAN YOU TELL? SO
LET ME HOLD YOU CLOSE IN HEART. IN TIME I WILL BRING YOU
PRIDE. A MOTHERS WISH COME TRUE.. FROM
THE CHILD YOU HELD INSIDE, THE STEPS
THAT I'M NOW TAKING, THEY'RE LEADING BACK
YOUR WAY. WE WILL ALWAYS LOVE YOU MOM..
HAPPY MOTHERS DAY.

YOU AND I-

BY:

LYDELL KING

EVERY TIME I WISH UPON A STAR, MY WISHES
BEGIN WITH YOUR NAME, I KNOW THE DISTANCE
BETWEEN US IS FAR, I'M SO GLAD YOU CAME.

THIS WORLD CAN BE A HARD PLACE STEEL,
CONCRETE, AND RAZER WIRE. COPS SUITED
UP CARRYING MACE, HOWEVER NOTHING CAN
PUT OUT THIS SOUL FIRE!
ON OUR MOMENTS I OFTEN REMINISCE, MY ARMS
AROUND YOU THERE'S SO MUCH I MISS,
WHY WAS I SUCH A FOOL.,

IRON GATES SLAM AT SPECIFIC TIMES, REMINDING
ME OF MY REALITY, TRYING HARD FOR SUBLIME,
WHAT A PLACE TO BE.
HEARING YOUR VOICE ON THE PHONE, SWEET MUSIC
TO MY EARS, MY DREAMS OF YOU ALWAYS EQUAL
HOME BRAKING DOWN INSIDE, HIDING MY TEARS..

SIT AWAY-

BY:
LAYCELLE KING

WHO SAYS THE SEA CAN'T MOVE IN WINTER,
OR THE CLOUDS STAND STILL IN A STORM.
WHO SAYS A MAN CAN'T CRY AND BE ALONE.
WHO SAYS A MAN CAN'T TEND TO BE BORED.
AND IF YOU COULD SEE INSIDE MY HEART YOU
WOULD SEE A LOT OF HURT. AND IF I COULD SHOW YOU
MY MIND, YOU WOULD SEE THE STRESS,
AND YOU WOULD SEE WHY I SIT AWAY, ALONE.
SO I GATHER MY THINGS AND BE ON MY WAY,
INTO MY ALONE PLACE, WHICH I CALL MY CELL,
I'M FEELING LONELY AND ALL ALONE, AND JUST
NEED TO GET AWAY.
IF YOU COULD KNOW WHAT I'M AFRAID
OF YOU WOULD BE FRIGHTENED.
IF YOU COULD FEEL AND SEE THE PAIN
THAT I FEEL, THEN YOU WOULD
TRULY KNOW WHY I SIT AWAY.
I GET AWAY ONLY IN MY MIND. I GET AWAY ALONE,
NOW SOME TIME I FEEL LIKE I'M NOT LOVED.

AS WE WALK-

BY:
LAYCELLE KING

ALL ALONE THERE WE WERE,
WALKING HAND AND HAND,
ON THE BEACH, IN THE SAND.
OUR HEARTS RACE,
AS I HOLD YOU TIGHT, THUNDER BOOMS,
AS THE LIGHTING STRIKE! HOLD YOU CLOSE,
FOR I KNOW YOU, YOU ARE SCARRED.
YOU TELL ME YOU LOVE ME, I SAY IT
TOO. OUR HEARTS WONDER,
IS THIS LOVE OR IS IT DOOM? AS THE TIDE ROLLS IN,
WE ARE SWEPT AWAY IN EACH OTHER, AS WE
MAKE LOVE, THE SAND SLJPS AWAY.
OUR NIGHT OF PASSION, TELLS ME THE TRUTH,
YOU ARE FOR ME, AS I AM FOR YOU.
I MUST GO FOR NOW, HOWEVER I WILL BE BACK,
THIS I WILL STICK TOO.

DREAMS OF YOU-

BY:
LAYCELLE KING

I'LL DO ANYTHING TO SPEND A UTILE TIME WITH YOU,
THE WAY YOU TURN MY WORLD ALL AROUND,
FEELS SO GOOD.

WHEN I GO TO SLEEP, LATE AT NIGHT, ALL I SEE
GIRL IS YOU, BABY YOU BLOW MY MIND. WHAT
AM I SUPPOSE TO DO? ALL I WANT IS YOU TO LOOK
INTO MY EYES AND TELL ME WHAT I'M GOING THROUGH.

YOU MIGHT SEE SOMETHING THAT YOU LIKE,
A PARADISE FOR TWO. SO WON'T YOU TAKE A LITTLE TIME,
NOW THAT YOU KNOW HOW I FEEL.
I DON'T NEED NO LIE DETECTOR TO SEE I'M FOR REAL,
I WANT YOU BAD. WHEN I'M DREAMING ABOUT YOU,
GIRL YOU ARE ONE OF A KIND, I WISH
THAT YOU WERE MY BABY.

LET ME-

BY:
LAYCELLE & SHANNON KING

LET ME TASTE YOUR LUCIONS LIPS,
FROM EACH OTHER WE CAN TAKE TIPS.
SIT WITH ME SHANNON ON THIS GOLDEN SAND,
LAY RIGHT HERE AND TAKE MY HAND LAYCELLE.
LOOK UP AT THE BEAUTIFUL BLUE SKY MY QUEEN,
I WANT YOU AND I CAN TELL YOU WANT ME MY KING,
CAUSE I KNOW US TWO WAS MEANT TO BE.
FEEL THE SOFTNESS OF MY TOUCH MY QUEEN?
AS I MAKE YOU FEEL LIKE CHOCOLATE DUTCH.
I WILL RUN MY FINGERS THROUGH YOUR HAIR
MY QUEEN, RELIEVING YOU FROM ANY
HEART ACHING DESPAIR.
TOGETHER WE CAN HOLD EACH OTHER TIGHT,
FROM MORNING UNTIL NEXT DAWN'S EARLY NIGHT.
YOU LISTEN AS MY HEART BEATS, AS I FEEL ALL
OF YOUR BODY'S HEAT.
I WANT TO BE THE ONE THAT YOU LOVE, TOGETHER
WE WILL STAY LIKE TWO DOVES.

CAUGHT UP IN LOVE-

BY: LAYCELLE KING

THE GODDESS OF MY LOVE
YOU ARE TO ME.
YOU CAPTURED MY HEART,
AND SET ME FREE.
CAUGHT IN THE MIDDLE,
BETWEEN NIGHT AND DAY.

I NEVER KNEW LOVE COULD
HOLD YOU THAT WAY,
FREE LIKE THE WIND,
MYSTERIOUS AS THE SEA.

MORE PRECIOUS THAN LIFE,
IS YOUR SMILE TO ME.
WITH EYES THAT SPARKLE,
LIKE GEMS OF THE EAST,
WITH A LOVE SO TENDER,
SHE LOVED THIS MAN CALLED BEAST.

KEEP YOUR ROSE ALIVE-

BY:
LAYCELLE KING

LONELY I THE QUEEN WHILE YOUR KING HAS GONE AWAY,"
LOVELY IS YOUR HEART THAT RADIATES EVERY DAY, MEMORIES
OF US WASH ACROSS THE SEAS OF TIME, STRONG IS THE ROSE.

INVINCIBLE IS THE VINE, PRIDE IN GENTLE WAYS,
UNKNOWN TO MAN, STRENGTHENS YOUR RESOLVE
IN FAITH, AND STEADIES YOUR NOBLE HAND,

QUEEN OF LOVE, YOUR HEART IS PURE AND THIS
MUCH SHOULD YOU KNOW. EVEN IN THE DARKEST
HOURS, YOUR ROSE IT STILL DOES GROW.

RISING UP THROUGH YOUR DREAMS, YOUR KING
FEELS IT'S WARMTH UNFOLD, MANY ARE THE MY
STORIES AND BEAUTIES OF THIS ROSE.

ONE DAY SOON YOUR KING WILL COME RETURNING
TO YOUR SHORE, SHURE OF IT, SO KEEP YOUR ROSE
ALIVE, FOR OF IT'S LOVE I CAN BE SURE.

MY NORTHERN STAR-

BY:
LAYCELLE KING

I SAW YOU ENTER FROM AFAR, TO ME YOU
WHERE THE NORTHERN STAR.

AS I GAZED AT YOU THAT NIGHT, MY SENSES FELT
SUPREME DELIGHT. YOU DID NOT SEE ME WATCHING
YOU, YET THIS I DID THE WHOLE NIGHT THROUGH.

EVERYTHING AROUND YOU COULD NOT COMPETE,
COULD NOT COMPARE. IN THAT INSTANT OF FIRST
SIGHT, I FELT THE STING OF LOVES FIRST BITE.

I WAS A VOYAGER IN SPACE, MY GUIDING LIGHT WAS
YOUR LOVELY FACE. IN ALL YOUR RADIANT GLORY BRIGHT,
I WATCHED YOU MOVE THROUGH OUT THE NIGHT.

PHONEING YOU-

BY:
LAYCELLE KING

AS I SIT HERE THINKING ABOUT YOU, I RUN TO THE PHONE.
DIAL YOUR NUMBER, BUT YOU ARE NOT HOME. AS I HANG
UP, CRAZY THOUGHTS RUN THROUGH MY MIND.

KNOWING ALL ALONG, I CAN'T CONTROL NOTHING
BEHIND STILL. YET I STILL SAY YOUR MINE. I GO
BACK TO MY CELL WANTING TO TELL YOU HOW
YOU GOT MY MIND GOING THROUGH HELL.

IN REALITY IT'S MY HELL THAT GOT ME HERE, I HAVE TO TAKE
THE HEAT UNTIL WE MEAT. SO I DON'T REPEAT, WHAT I DID
IN THE STREETS, SO NOW WHEN I CALL YOU ON THE PHONE
AND YOUR NOT HOME, I DON'T MOEN OR GROAN.

I JUST HANG UP THE PHONE AND DON'T LET IT BE
KNOWN THAT I FEEL SO ALONE INSIDE...

"LOVING A MAN IN PRISON"

BY:

unknown

LOVING A MAN IN PRISON IS NOT ALWAYS EASY TO DO..
LOVING ONE HAS A HIGH PRICE TO PAY..
IT MEANS BEING YOUNG, YET FEELING OLD..
IT'S WRITING HIS AND YOUR LOVE
TO EACH OTHER, AND SAYING I LOVE YOU TOO,..
A KISS BY PHONE, A PROMISE TO WAIT,
KNOWING THE PAROLE BOARD HAS HIS RELEASE
DATE HOLDING IN THEIR FATE..
IT'S RELUCTANTLY PAINFUL LETTING HIM GO.
IT'S HURTING INSIDE, NEEDING HIM SO.
IT'S FEELING HIS PAIN, EYES FILLED WITH TEARS...
IT'S BEING ALONE WITH YOUR HOPES, DREAMS
AND TEARS FOR SO MANY YEARS...
IT'S BEING NEAR, YET SO FAR AWAY.
YOU'RE LOVING HIM MORE WITH EACH PASSING DAY
LOVING HIM SAYS JUST WHAT IT MEANS..
WEEKS TURN INTO MONTHS,
MONTHS SEEM LIKE YEARS... LOVING A MAN IN PRISON MEANS
SHEDDING MANY TEARS...
THERE WILL BE AN ADDED LOVE ONCE HISTIME IS DONE...
HOWEVER ONLY THROUGH FAITH IN YOUR HEART
WILL OUR BATTLE BE WON

SHANNON-

BY:
LAYCELLE KING

BEAUTIFUL SHANNON, WOMAN OF MY LIFE,
YOU PUT A MOJO ON ME. YOU ARE TRULY A
MOST PLEASANT SIGHT FOR THIS MAN TO SEE.
TURNING YOUR GAZE BOLDLY BACK INTO MINE.
KNOWING SURENESS, WE ARE ONE OF A KIND.
YOUR SPELLBINDING GAZE HAS TAKEN HOLD OF MY SOUL.
COMPELLING OUR LOVE TO SUBMIT, REFUSING
TO LET GO AND UPON YOUR FACE ALIGHTS THE
SEXIEST OF SMILES AN APPROVAL OF DEEP PASSION,
LETTING ME KNOW YOU LIKE MY STYLE,
WITHIN THE NIGHT WE ARE DREAM
COMPARING OF SECRET DESIRES,
WE'LL FOREVER BE SHARING, YOU ARE MY SUGAR -N-
SPICE, MY CUP OF TEA, MY QUEEN WHO KNOWS
HOW TO PLEASE ME.
YOUR WONDERING PASSION IS TRULY
A BLISS, YES NOTHING COMPARES TO THE LOVE I GET FROM
MY QUEEN...

LOVE GAME-

BY:
LAYCELLE KING

MANY IS THE TIME,
I THOUGHT IT WAS LOVE.
SOON I FOUND I WAS WRONG.

ONLY TO PICK UP MY HEART AGAIN.
THIS GAME I'LL NEVER WIN,

HOWEVER I KEEP PLAYING.
SO MANY HOLLOW PROMISES,

AND SHATTERED DREAMS,
HOLDING IT TIGHT INSIDE.

EMPTY EYES SEARCHING WITH EVERY
SOFT CARESS, SEEKING TO FULFILL,

THE NEED TO KNOW, AND URGE TO EXPLORE
SMILES ALWAYS DECEIVING, FOR THERE'S
NO RULES TO THIS GAME.

FOR THE LOVE OF YOU

BY:
LAYCELLE KING

I'VE WALKED THE LONGEST MILE IN THE DESERTS SUN,
AND HAVE SWAM THE COLDEST ANTARCTICA OCEAN.
THOUGH MY FEET HURT, MY BODY IS COLD WITHIN,
I STILL CLIMBED THE HIGHEST WALL AND
HURDLE THE TALLEST FENCE.
MY FEELINGS IS NOT NO MERE COINCIDENCE.
AS THE TIME LIE ON MY HEART FILL WITH PAIN.
WITH OUT YOU, NO MORE TOO LOSE, NO MORE
TO GAIN. SO TELL ME, IS IT TRUE WHAT THEY SAY?
DO THE PAIN STICK AROUND OR SOON GO AWAY.
YES IT'S KILLING ME SOFTLY, THE THINGS THAT I
DO. YET UNTIL THE DAY I DIE, IT WILL DO, NOT
FOR ME, BUT FOR THE LOVE OF YOU.

DEEP DARK LOVE-

BY:
LAYCELLE KING

WHY DO I NEED YOU SO? YOUR DEEP DARK LOVE,
BLOOD MIXED WITH EVIL POISON,
NEED TO FEEL YOU DEEP, SO DEEP INSIDE MY
BONES. NEED YOUR RUSH, NEED
YOUR THRILL, ALTHOUGH MASS INJECTIONS KILL,
WHY DO I NEED YOU SO?
YOUR DEEP DARK LOVE, LOVE OR LUST CAN'T HANDLE THIS,
HOWEVER I NEED
YOU SO, HOLD ME, THRILL ME, EVEN IF A MOMENTS
PLEASURE KILLS ME.
WHY DO I NEED YOU SO? YOUR DEEP DARK LOVE,
CAN'T DIE, NOT YET, LIFE WAS
SO NEW. COULD NOT TELL, DIDN'T KNOW THE
WICKET SECRET YOU HOLD HIV,
YOUR LOVES SILENT GIFT TO ME.

"I WALK DOWN THIS LONELY ROAD ON MY OWN"

+ ◆ ◆ ◆ ◆ +

BY:
LAYCELLE KING

I WALK DOWN THIS LONELY ROAD ON MY OWN.
TEARS FALLING, FALLING DOWN THE TRIAL OF
FRUSTRATION INTO THE DEPTHS OF LONELINESS.
I WALK DOWN THIS LONELY ROAD ON MY OWN.
FACES BLURRING, BLURRING IN THE MISTS OF
CONFUSION INTO THE DEPTHS OF SUB CONSCIOUSNESS.
I WALK DOWN THIS LONELY
ROAD ON MY OWN. DESIRES BURNING, BURNING
DOWN THE WALLS OF MY EMOTIONS INTO THE
DEPTHS OF MY HEART.

WORDS

BY:
LAYCELLE KING

I WRITE THESE WORDS IN PLACE OF MY TEARS.
THE WORDS FLOW, FLOODING THE PAPER, LIKE
DROPS OF RAIN, HEALING THE EARTH, HEALING
MY HEART, HEALING MY SPIRIT, NEVER ENDING
WORDS.

"I PAINTED A MASK"

BY: LAYCELLE KING

A MASK CAN HIDE ALL THE TRUTHS ONE DOES

NOT WANT TO BE SEEN.

A MASK CAN HIDE ALL THE EMOTIONS ONE DOES

NOT WANT TO BE FELT.

A MASK CAN HIDE ALL THE THINGS ONE
DOES NOT WANT TO BELIEVE.

A MASK CAN HIDE ALL THESE THINGS, HOWEVER
CANNOT STOP THEM FROM BEING REAL.

I PAINTED A MASK TO HIDE ALL MY EMOTIONS. I

PAINTED A MASK TO HIDE ALL MY FEARS.
I PAINTED A MASK HOWEVER COULD NOT
HIDE FROM MYSELF.

PIERCED SOUL -

BY:
LAYCELLE KING

MY SOUL IS BEAT UP, IT'S BATTERED, HOWEVER
IT SEEMS TO EVERY ONE ELSE
IT DOESN'T MATIER..
I'VE BEEN SHOT MANY TIMES IN MY SOUL,
IT SEEMS NOW, MY BODY NEVER GOES COLD,
FOR I FOREVER HAVE A PIERCED SOUL..

I'M AMAZED I'M STILL BREATHING, IT SEEMS MY
SOUL IS TEAZING MY HEART WHICH IS STEAL.

IF YOU FELT FOR AN HOUR, MY SOULS PAIN,
IT WOULD DRIVE YOU INSANE. IN THE BRAIN AND
PUT STRAIN ON THE VEINS IN YOUR MEMBRANE.
AS I WALK DOWN THIS LONELY PIERCED
SOUL LANE, I HAVE A PIERCED SOUL NOW FOREVER
AND A DAY. NOW IT SEEMS MY HEART WON'T
MAKE ANOTHER DAY..
FOR THE STRAIN OF A PIERCED SOUL IS TOO GREAT,
I'M SURE IT'S ABOUT TO CARRY ME OFF TO MY
DEATH DATE, WHICH IS NOW CONSIDERED
MY FATE, A PIERCED SOUL...

BALL & CHAIN-

BY:
LAYCELLE KING

THE THINGS I DRAG AROUND,
ALWAYS EFFECT MY BRAIN,
AND THE PAIN I SUSTAIN,
WILL ALWAYS MAINTAIN,

WEIGHING HEAVILY UPON ME,
LIKE A BALL AND CHAIN.
I NEVER STOP DRESSING MY
THOUGHTS WITH CLOTHS OF

EMOTIONS IN WHICH I SOUGHT.
AS I SIT AND PLOT HOW TO
FREE MYSELF, PLAYING MENTAL
GAMES IN MY BRAIN.
STRAINING TO END THE GAME,
I REALIZE I'M FOREVER LOCKED
TO THIS BALL AND CHAIN.

"ALONE"

BY:
LAYCELLE KING

Here alone with memories of a friend. locked away behind the physical walls of prison. Silent times when the memories begin to fade, I cling to the memory of how we spent our days. I wonder some days about the grave and these walls, is there any differences in the two, a spiritual connection of hope, those things shared by few. Here alone I sit, with memories of a friend... Moving between the shadows of fear, loneliness and doubt. Holding to the memories of my friend, while seeking to find a real way out.

A WOMAN'S WORTH

A woman is a man's best treasure, the earths
stability to keep producing what's golden.
Any true King knows a Queens worth this here
Alone will keep a relationship strong as well as
Wistful.
The world is full of complications, mental brake
Downs and physical games, yet the love of a
True woman and man will overcome all this.
The love we share will continue to help us
Through all the games as well as test the
World throw our way.
We are the true merchants of our destiny,
The true holders of our soul as I am that
True king that will make it all right in your Life.

BY: LYDELL KING
1-22-03

STANDING

When you have stood on the shores of your own
Soul and watched the tide of change ebb and flow:
When you have stood alone in the midst of doubt
And confusion, in witness of your own tears and
Pain. Once you travel the path of your soul
And the longing of your cosmic spirit.
This day have I saw you in the midst of my soul.
I have held you in the vision of yesterday and
Today. This day have I understood the real rhythm
Of life and knew again myself. Wind swept dreams
Upon the conscious soul touched again and again
By the cosmic flow of time. This day have I
Held you in the midst of my soul. Feeling the true
Essence of your spiritual being. Love is not woven
Flowers or superficial promises of the flesh.
True Love is movement in the stillness of the soul...
The silence that hears your need.
When you have stood on the shores of your own
Soul and understood the view of that which you
See. Then and only then will you move into the
Knowledge of self... Then the real dance of life
And love began...

BY: LAYCELLE KING

SOFTLY SPOKEN

Softly spoken, I find myself provoked..softly
Spoken I find myself choked upon my own
Thoughts. Softly spoken my mouth speaks with
Thunder and at times the devil takes me under,
Cause I'm full of hunger or should I say thunder.
We all are racing against death, for it shall
Profess our birth and, how long we are on
This earth. How can I introduce you to this
Pain that I maintain in my brain. Softly
As I sleep my freedom has been kept.
Hidden beyond these walls which is surely
Going to remain tall. As my dreams began
To fall, I began to see it all. Crumbling
Like chips my thoughts began to slip.
Softly as my soul dips my mind feels like
A fist, strong at time, yet soft with time.

By: LYDELL KING

FACE- 2- FACE

I dedicate this to the day we
Finally meet face to face.
I've waited for this day to
Come for so long.
No more do I have to pretend
Your presence is close to home,
For here you are staring me in
My eyes, close within my reach.
I wish our time together could
Last forever. I never want to
Leave your side. But although I
Cannot stay in your arms, I
Will forever stay. in your heart.
And that my love, is where
I Carry you every day.

By: LAYCELLE KING

THE VISION

A vision of you is all I
See at night and all I want
To do is reach out and hold
You tight, for you are the light
That helps me see again through
This dark world that has seemed
To take over the night. With
You and I as a team, as one
We can overcome anything,
Day or night cause with us
It's on, on sight and that's
How it's suppose to go down
When you have truly found
Your soul mate to fight the
Battle which goes on every
Day and night in this game
They call life.

BY: LYDELL KING

MY LADY

Pretty eyes that sparkle and
Shine, a beautiful lady. I'm so
Glad you are mine, long hair,
Smooth silky skin, I know I'm
In love but that not a sin.
I pray for a life with the kids,
You and me living together,
Happy as can be. A nice big
Yard, weather it's easy,
Weather it's hard I'll be there
For you night and day. I'm
Your forever with you, I'll
Stay...

By: LAYCELLE KING

LAST NIGHT

Last night I closed my eyes and saw a heavenly figure
Before me, a sweet kind; gentle creature.. I walked

Closer I was so drawn to it as I approached, the scent
Of this creature was invigorating the touch was erotic.

I looked deeper and it was you. You pulled me closer
Breathing in my scent caressing my soul with your
Words, and journeying across my body with your eyes.
A lingering glance at my lips you lean into me tasting
Them, the sweetness enthralled you. I feel the desire
In your touch the excitement in your stare you whisper
To me the mere sound of your every breath takes hold
Of my soul..

BY: LYDELL KING

"YOUR COMFORT"

I missed the times we used to share,
My love was all I had to spare, I
Had this feeling deep in my mind,
That we could stay together till
The end of time, I think in the
Day and dream in the night, that
The love we shared will reunite,
Maybe it will and maybe it won't
Life goes on and we'll both know,
There's a place in my heart that's
Warm and true, If you ever need
Someone to comfort you, remember
That place that's open only to you..

BY: LAYCELLE KING

THE WALLS ARE CLOSING IN

The walls are closing in, time is running out and my
Patience is running thin from within. I look at my
Surroundings, there is enough pain, suffering and
Agony to make any man in his right mind go insane.
I have endured this since the ripe age of 15, yet
I think to myself, is it my time and place to go
Insane, for the walls are closing in.
I can't let my family down, for they have endured
Enough already, yet the walls are closing in. What am
suppose to do, caught in the belly of the beast with
The devil tapping at my mind with all it's might.
Now I think to myself am I suppose to fight it like
The warrior I am? Or do I continue to let the walls
Close in and hope that I will become another soul that
Blends in, so I am able to see the end of the walls
That's closing in..

BY: LYDELL KING

SADNESS

BY:
LAYCELLE KING

Searching for the path that will lead the way
To a happiness known in former days tormented
Knowing that the way is paved in my mind, however
Is blocked by a slew of wretched pain, my love is
Weakened by the sorrow of emptiness felt through
Loneliness of the state for which I'm in for yesterday's
Memories are only etched of a life that has passed...
Away. Color has faded leaving dull feelings toward
Emotions of strife inflicted upon my heart yet,
Tomorrow may be the time for which I yearn, that
Will bring warmth from the rays of elation, though
The love that remains in my heart brings to me a
State of contentment for all of whom I care, It is
Only he who can repair all damages caused by me, or
Aimed at me by these tears from my eyes..

OF CONVICTS

BY:
LYDELL KING

Behind the walls in a prison enclosure, hidden there
From public exposure, men endure filth and human brutality,
where nightmares exist in cruel reality.

Treated like animals, cheated and abused,
our talents and skills shamefully used,
where sadistic guards exercise them, then
condoned by superiors who encourage them.

Every day in prison, in a convicts life is made to be one
of strife, where in we are doomed to forever be,
The hopeless victim of misery.

Here in a world of bitterness and sorrow,
men live and curse their tomorrows
enduring a torment made harder
To bear by the knowledge that society don't care.

For we are criminals, it's understandable true, yet
we are also human too, and being humans we
deserve to be treated much more humanly..

THOUGHTS

BY
LAYCELLE KING

Thoughts of you in my head
Before I lay to go to bed.

Thoughts of you and me
Which makes everything

Coo. Thoughts of you in
My mind and those thoughts

Are so divine. Thoughts of
Many plans that involves lots

Of time. Can you see these
Thoughts too?

YOU ALREADY KNOW

BY:
LYDELL KING

You already know just how I feel about
You. I had a dream one day and I knew

It came true because I have found a real
Love, you already know. It's forever you

And I, so keep it real with your man, it's
Us against the world. I'm tryin to hold

On forever so we will always stay together
My boo bear, my lover there will never

Be another who can love you like I can,
I'm speaking to you my lover my friend.

IN YOUR HANDS

BY:
LAYCELLE KING

In your hands be hold the ancient scroll which hold
The words of this lost man's soul..
Many tails have be told about this scroll, however
It's never been unrolled..
The day I was born I was already convicted of a crime
Of having bars around my mind..
Within this scroll I'm trapped in the belly of hell..

In my mind gun shots blast and many minds laugh..
I feel the draft of yesterday's laughs which bring in
Today's misshappens...
Slowly chipping away at my brain
is this never ending Pain..

This pain easily manifest it's way into my veins which
Bring in a heart full of rain which drains my sanity...
The pain within me is the pain beyond me, that's why

It's poured upon me and not in my hands...
For if it's your hands you can release me from
This scroll and send me home within this poem...

LOVE

BY:
LYDELL KING

The most beautiful things in life are not visible to the human eye. Take love for instance. You cannot see love, nor can you touch it, yet it is a very wonderful part of life. To love another person you must love yourself first, and if you love yourself, you also love your higher power. Because your higher power made you. The feeling of love is in the heart and mind. That's where real love dwell.. Real love is not in the physical aspect, nor characteristics.

If you happen to find real love.. not a so called love filled with mind games and confusion. Then hold onto it. Because love can get you through any problem. Love can help people in times of need, love can also better people, most importantly yourself. The higher power made love for a reason, so every one can come together and feel wanted, and appreciated by someone. Every one deserves to be loved, so if you do find that love in your life time hang on to it, because love is a very vary special part of life and even in the after life.

PASSING THROUGH

BY:
LAYCELLE KING

Passing through these prison gates, have me
Wondering about my life, my prolonged death
Date... You see demons surround me all the
Time. It's as if screaming, tormented souls,
Hold captive my mind, and I'm passing through
Hell, with one foot already in the grave. It's as

If I'm a slave to these forever lost black days..
How could I ever hope when hope becomes a rope

Dancing around my neck causing my life to become
A fatal wreck.. Dramatic emotions pass through my
Mind leaving me with thoughts of executions entwined
Like vines in my fragile mind.. If eyes could hear
What would they listen too? If souls could speak,
What would they say? Would they forever be
Consumed with pain and dismay, or would they
Let the thought and sound of life fade like yesterday..

WHEN YOU FEEL THE NEED

BY:
LYDELL KING

WHEN TIMES GET TOUGH THINK ABOUT ME.
BABY YOU CAN NEVER DO IT ENOUGH, I
FEEL YOUR PAIN AS YOU FEEL MINE, YOU
FEEL MINE, YOU KNOW WHAT THAT MEANS?
TRUE SOUL MATES DIVINE YOU CAN CALL
ON ME WHEN YOU FEEL TH NEED.
MORE LOVE THEN I'VE EVER KNOWN,
I CAN'T WAIT TILL THE DAY I COME
HOME, I MISS YOU BABY MORE AND
MORE EACH DAY, I KNOW FOR A
FACT OUR LOVE IS HERE TO STAY,
FROM MY PROPOSAL ON BENDED
KNEE, CRY ON MY SHOULDER
WHEN YOU FEEL THE NEED.
I KNOW OUR SITUATION AT THIS
TIME DOES NOT MAKE US HAPPY,
YET IN DUE TIME THEY CAN'T
MAKE U OR BRAKE US OUR LOVE
I TP STRONG THEY ARE TESTING
OUR FAITH AND TRYING TO PROVE
US WRONG.

"THE BURNING NEED FOR MY TWIN BROTHER"

BY:

LAYCELLE KING

My twin bother I've been so depressed, some nights I ponder, some nights I wander... in a land that seems engrossed in death... Bro it's my souls distress...

Makes me hate the world, makes my hate eternal..

Sure it'll make my soul not rest...

Obsessed with the thought of why I took two peoples lives.. the murder rate being high, fear in those I'm making hurt and cry ... those who felt exempt choices that consist of reason amidst my forever feeding demons... Creations who attempt to shame, attempt to gain but face over whelming opposition... got no pot to piss in bro, please stop and listen... my twin brother oh when I complain, I know it weighs heavy on you like a 20 ton train... thank you so very much for having so much patience this time is heavy for us both... by your example I am able to cope and keep from putting rope around throat... choke and hang... covered in fescues end my pain and guilt known to eliminate my species... what kind of man lay's under anger and passive expression, guessing they will never understand... that I didn't have a real father figure but my twin... for I got some thing to prove... with a life time full of gratitude, we will never lose... still my emotions are not wear that war vest... with a Tee in each of my minds eye, hit or miss... till there's nothing left... please rest my for ever wondering and heavy guilty soul...

DREAMS

BY:
LYDELL KING

Dreams from my heart
Thoughts of you in my
Mind feelings for you
In my heart,my skin,
Tingles from your touch.
My lips tremble from
Your kisses my head
Is spinning from your
Whispers my heart is
Beating fast from your
Words, is this the dream
Of all dreams?

"PRISON CELL"

8-11-2004
BY:
LAYCELLE KING

As the lights in my small prison cell
start to dim and then go off...
My thoughts start to really run amuck..
For this I the only time I have to truly think without
being interrupted by any one or anything...
As time continue to be my friend and ally instead of my
enemy, sentiments of my new found man hood begin
to blossom then shine...
As I close my now tired eyes, thoughts come rushing
in the fluid gates of my subconchense like a action
movie... I think to myself where do I begin?
No sooner hat I think that the answer hits me, there
is no beginning to a never ending story...

RAINBOW

BY:
LYDELL KING

A RAINBOW MAKES A PRIMISS
THAT LIFE IS HERE TO STAY,
PROMISE MEANS THERE'S MORE
TO LIFE THAN WHAT WE KNOW TODAY.
WE CAN SHARE TOMORROW IF

THERES ONE TO PLEDGE IT TO,
I WOULD LOVE TO BE THE RAINBOW
WHO PROMISSES LOVE TO YOU.

AS I LOOK AT MYSELF IN A BROKEN MIRROR

BY:
LAYCELLE KING

AS I LOOK AT MYSELF IN THIS BROKEN MIRROR, I SEE A FACE
FULL OF PAIN AND STRAIN THAT'S LOOKING BACK AT ME,
BEGGING ME TO RELEASE IT'S LIFE CHANGING PAIN..
AS I LOOK INTO THIS BROKEN MIRROR I SEE THROUGH
THE MANY SPLINTERED MIRRORS ALL THE YEARS
WASHED AWAY ALL MY NEVER CRIED TEARS..
AS I LOOK INTO THIS BROKEN MIRROR IT BRINGS
UP AND BRINGS BACK ALL MY FEARS WHICH I'VE
COVERED UP AND MASKED WITH SNEARS...
TO MY SURPRISE THIS MIRROR SHOWS ALL OF MY PAIN,
HURT, CONFUSION, MISUNDERSTANDINGS, SHORT
COMINGS AND MY INSECURITIES JUST TO NAME A FEW..
ONE THING THAT IS TRUE IS PAIN, GUILT AND
DISAPPOINTMENT SEEM TO RUN THIS BODY OF MINE..
LEAVING MY SANITY AND LOVE BEHIND...

AS I TRY TO UNDERSTAND WHAT ALL THIS
BROKEN MIRROR IS SHOWING ME. IT'S AS IF I
AM FROZE WITHIN MY CURRENT REALITY...
RIGHT BEFORE MY VERY EYES, MY FACE TURNS INTO A
IMAGE I AM NOT FAMILYER WITH SEEING. IT BECOMES CLEAR
NOW, I AM STILL TRYING TO FIGURE LAYCELLE OUT...

MOMMA I APOLOGIZE

BY:
LYDELL & LAYCELLE KING

MOM THIS IS A POEM OF APOLOGY FOR
ALL OUR WRONG DOINGS..
MOM AS WE SIT HERE IN THE RAIN THE RAIN DROPS
DROP A THOUSAND TIMES OUR SORROW, OUR PAIN..
MOMMA WE APOLOGIZE FOR ALL THE TEARS WE LEAVE IN
YOUR EYES.. MOMMA WE APOLOGIZE FOR ALL THE SILENT
CRIES. MOMMA WE APOLOGIZE FOR HAVING YOU GO
THROUGH THIS PHYSICAL INCARCERATION WITH US.
MOMMA WE APOLOGIZE FOR BEING THE ONE WHO
BROKE YOUR OH SO DELICATE HEART WITH OUR FAILURES..
MOMMA WE APOLOGIZE FOR NOT BEING THOSE SONS
THAT GLEAM IN YOUR EYE... MOMMA WE APOLOGIZE FOR
BEING THAT MAN AT TIMES YOU SO RESENT, MY FATHER...

MOMMA WE APOLOGIZE, WE KNOW THAT TIMES HAS BEEN
RUFF, OR YEARS WE SHOULD SAY, TIME HAS PAST AND
NONE OF IT HAS BEEN FAKE. WE ARE READY TO SHAKE THIS
FICTITIOUS HOME AND COME HOME TO OUR REAL HOME...
MOMMA WE APOLOGIZE FOR ALL THE PAIN WE
HAVE DONE, WE WANT THE TRUE TREE BACK
TOGETHER AS ONE, MOMMA WE APOLOGIZE...

91

ONCE HAD YOUR LOVE IN MY HAND

BY:
LYDELL KING

YOU ONCE SAID I HAD YOUR HEART, NOW
YOUR GONE AND I'M TORN APART.
WHAT HAPPENED WHAT WENT WRONG? YOU WHERE
THERE ONCE NOW YOUR GONE, CAN'T LOOK YOU IN
THE FACE TOO AFRAID IT WILL SHOW I'VE BEEN MISSING
YOU SO MUCH MORE THEN YOU WILL EVER KNOW..
ONCE I WAS YOURS AND YOU MINE, NOW I'M
ALL ALONE, IT'S WORSE THEN DOING TIME.
THINGS HAPPEN, GOTTA BE STRONG, YOU WERE THERE ONCE,
NOW YOUR GONE CAN'T BEGIN TO COMPREHEND IT.
BELIEVE ME I TRY, WHAT CAN I DO, WHATS ON YOUR MIND,
ONCE WE WHERE FRIENDS, ONCE WE WHERE LOVERS, ONCE
THERE WAS TO BE NO OTHER, BUT THINGS HAPPEN, GOTTA
BE STRONG, YOU WAS THERE ONCE, NOW YOUR GONE.

SHATTERED DREAMS ENGULFED IN SHACKLED MEMORIES

BY:
LAYCELLE KING

THE VERY FIRST DAY I WALKED THROUGH THESE
PRISON GATES I FELT THIS PLACE EMBRACE MY
VERY YOUNG FATE...
THE SHADOWS OF THIS PRISON LIFE IS SLOWLY
CLOSING IN ON MY VERY YOUNG LIFE...
I CAN FEEL THE PRESSURE AND THE WEIGHT PUSHIN
HARD ON MY THROAT BOX..
THROUGH THIS WHOLE ORDEAL, I'VE TAKEN A LONG
WALK BESIDE MY RAW EMOTIONS... GETTING TO
KNOW SELF, SOME THINGS PROVE TO BE A TRUE
JOB. MOST PEOPLE ARE STUCK AND PARPLIZED IN
THEIR OWN MINDS AND CAN'T CHANGE... SOME
THING I REFUSE TO DO. FOR I HAVE SHATTERED
DREAMS THAT ARE ENGULFED IN MY SHACKLED
MEMORIES OF ME BEING FREE..

93

DREAMS COME AND DREAMS GO

BY:
LYDELL KING

Dreams come and dreams go, loved
Ones come and some go, why does
Our life have so many wars? we pick
And we choose and most times we lose,
Those who win may never be so lucky
Again. Time after time I've made big
Mistakes, I've sold my life for a house
With the state, yes it's true I have three
Hots and a cot, yet it's not the life I want.
I ask this question time and time again, why
Does our life have so many wars? It's
Because dreams come and dreams go.

(AS I WAKE UP)

BY:
LAYCELLE KING

As I wake up in a cold sweat, a realization
Hit's me. I've invested 10 years plus this poem
In this prison life...

When it rains it's like I'm drowning in the
Lords pain... Or could it be my pain that's forever
Incased in chains...

Tear drops, drop from my painful eyes and fill
This page.. I feel my mind screaming a thousand
Times faster than yesterday...
A older and much wiser man once told me. To show your
pride is a sigh of a foolish man... The mind sees what the
heart only wants to feel... Most times I wish the world could
be engulfed in my pain... That way people wouldn't think I
was insane. However since they won't understand I hope I
can stay on land with my forever acing guilt and pain...

THE WEDDING VOWS

BY:
LYDELL KING

I'VE WAITED FOR A LIFE TIME
FOR THIS DAY TO COME, EVERY
SINCE I WAS ABLE TO LEARN.
NO MORE DO I HAVE TO PRETEND
THAT MY DREAM WOMAN IS JUST
A DREAM, FOR I AM FACE TO FACE
WITH YOU THIS SPECIAL DAY.
STARING ME IN MY EYES, CLOSE
WITHIN MY REACH, I TAKE AHOLD
OF YOUR HAND SO WE CAN TAKE
THAT TRIP IN MARRIAGE LAND.
AS YOU SOFTLY SAY I DO, WE
PASSIONATELY WALK THROUGH
THESE GOLDEN GATES THAT'S
MADE ONLY FOR YOU AND I.
ONCE, IN THE LAND OF LOVE, I SOFTLY GIVE YOU A KISS
THAT'S SENT FROM ABOVE. NOW THAT WE ARE ONE, ONE
TO BE I WILL FOREVER HOLD YOU IN MY HEART BECAUSE
YOU HAVE THE KEY AND THAT'S PLAIN TO SEE MY WIFEY

DEATH DEFINES THEE

BY:
LAYCELLE KING

HIDDEN BEYOND THESE CONCRETE WALLS YOU SHALL
FIND A MAN WHOES WELL INTACT IN THE MIND...
AT THE RIPE AGE OF 15 A BOY WAS LOCKED UP
FOR THE CRIME OF MURDER. UPON HIS ARRIVAL
TO PRISON HIS CURIOSITY HAD ARISEN...
RAZER WIRE AND METAL DOORS HAS BLURRED HIS
VISION. AS HE STEPS BACK MENTALLY TO GRASP IT ALL,
A VOICE IN HIS HEAD SAYS YOU AINT SEEN IT ALL...
AS THE YOUNG MAN IS LEAD DOWN A LONG COR
DOOR HE THINKS OF NOTHING ELSE BUT WHAT HE
IS HERE FOR. ONCE AMONG THE RAPES, ROBBERS
AND THUGS, HE KNOWS DEATH DEFINES THEE...
NOW AT THE AGE OF 22 0 THE STORIES HE COULD TELL HE'S
BEEN THROUGH. WALKING IN BETWEEN MENTAL BEAT DOWNS
AND MENTAL SLASHING, HE FINALLY REALIZE HE IS NOT ALIVE..
FOR THE DAY HE WAS SENTENCED TO LIFE PLUS 66 YEARS HE LOST
AND FORGOT ABOUT CRYING TEARS FOR DEATH DEFINES THEE...
WALKING AROUND THE TRACK TILL HIS FEET HURT HE THINKS
TO HIMSELF BEING ON THIS EARTH IS QUITE A CURSE...

FOR HE DOESN'T UNDERSTAND HOW GOD COULD BRING
HIM TO THIS LAND OF UNFORGOTTEN PLAINS AND HIMSELF
A MAN. HOLLOW DREAMS AN BROKEN PROMISES IS
ALL HE MAY EVER NEED FOR DEATH DEFINES THEE...

A WISH

———— ✦✦✦✦✦ ————

BY:
LYDELL KING

I START TO GET SENTIMENTAL
WHEN YOU COME TO MIND
YOUR BEAUTIFUL BLACK HAIR,
YOUR MYSTERIOUS BROWN EYES,
YOUR SHY DEMEANOR HIDING A
STRONG WOMAN INSIDE, LET HER
COME OUT, WHY DOES SHE HIDE?
RESPECTING YOUR INNER STRENGTH.
FROM THIS STEEL BED DREAMS OF
OUR FUTURE FAMILY GOING
THROUGH MY HEAD THEN
MY EYES OPEN AND I AWAKE
KEYS JINGLING SLAMMING GATES
I LOOK AROUND AND MY WALL COMES
BACK, REALITY SETS IN WITH ALL IT'S
WEIGHT GIVING NO SLACK, LIVING
IN A SITUATION THAT'S MAKE OR
BREAK YOU, STRIVING

TO NEVER BE BROKEN BY THOSE WHO
TAKE GETTING THROUGH EACH
DAY THE BEST WAY I CAN KEEPING MY GROWTH AT A STEADY
PACE WITH MY MIND INTACT INTO YOUR ARMS AND LIFE I'D
LIKE TO GO BACK.

(SCREAMS FROM THE SOUL)

BY:
LAYCELLE KING

AS I SIT DOWN AND WRITE THIS POEM
I'M SCREAMING FROM MY SOUL..
TIC TOC TIC TOC TIMES RUNNING OUT LIKE GRAIN
OF SAND PORING THROUGH MY HANDS...
THE PAIN, THE ANGER IN MY OWN MIND, HAS ME
SWINGING FROM VINES THROUGH OTHER
SHACKLED MINDS THAT ARE LEFT IN TIME,
FRAGMENTED MEMORIES SPREAD THROUGH
OUT MY MIND LEAVING ME BLIND SO I CAN'T
CLIMB THEM VINES WHICH HANG IN OTHERS MINDS...
AS I SIT IN THIS CELL, I'M GETTING OLD AND
MY SOUL IS TURNING COLD..
I'M SCREAMING FROM MY SOUL, HOWEVER IT
SEEMS THAT'S NO ONE HEARS ME.
MAY BE IT'S BECAUSE EVERY ONE FEARS ME...
STRATEGICALLY I MOVE SLOWLY AS I
BRUISE OTHERS WITH THE WORDS I CHOOSE,
I THINK TO MYSELF I HAVE NOTHING TO
LOOSE. FOR THE SCREAMS FROM
MY SOUL WILL NEVER GET OLD...

*****(AS THE WORLD TURN)*****

BY:
LYDELL KING

AS I THINK ABOUT HOW YOU LIVE
ME AND THE PROMISES YOU MAKE. I BRING
MYSELF TO THINK OF WAYS TO MAKE YOU
HAPPY DAY AFTER DAY. WHAT CAN I CHANGE
WHAT ISN'T RIGHT, I FEEL AS THOUGH I OWE
YOU MY LIFE. YOU HAVE CHANGED ME, IN SO
MANY WAYS, YOU'VE MADE ME THE MAN I AM
IN SO MANY WAYS, I LOVE YOU SO MUCH AND
YOUR LOVE I HAVE EARNED, PROMISE TO LOVE
ME TILL ETERNITY, AS THE WORLD TURNS.
IF YOU SHALL EVER GET DISCOURAGED, CALL
ON ME I'LL BE AROUND ALWAYS, KEEP YOUR HEAD
TO THE SKY, LET NO ONE GET YOU DOWN, OUR
LOVE IS ONE IN A MILLION, ON YOUR HEART I'VE
PLACED A CROWN, YOU ARE THE QUEEN IN MY
LIFE THE WOMAN TO WHICH I BELONG, YOU ARE
MY HEART, MY SOUL, MY ALL, MY SALVATION, MY EVERYTHING.
AS THE WORLD TURNS...

"WHERE I BELONG"

BY:
LAYCELLE KING

I LOVE TALKING WITH YOU,
HEART TO HEART,
HOWEVER I'M MISSING
BEING WITH YOU FACE TO FACE.
THIS IS SO HARD.
SOMETIMES OUR BEING APART
IS ALL I CAN THINK ABOUT.
I WISH I COULD WAVE A WOUND AND YOU
WILL MAGICALLY BE HERE,
RIGHT BY MY SIDE.
I WANT TO DO ALL THE THINGS
LOVERS DO. I WANT TO KISS YOUR LIPS,
HOLD YO TIGHT,
AND LOOK INTO YOUR EYES, THOSE BEAUTIFUL EYES.
TIME SEEM LIKE IT JUST CRAWLS
WHEN WE ARE AWAY FROM EACH
OTHER LIKE THIS.AS MUCH AS I LIKE TALKING WITH YOU,
I CAN'T WAIT UNTIL WE ARE TOGETHER
AGAIN BACK IN EACH OTHERS ARMS
WHERE WE BELONG..

(ELEMENTS OF YOUR BEING)

BY: LAYCELLE KING

ELEMENTS OF YOUR BEING ARE WHAT I'M SEEING..
ELEMENTS OF YOUR SOUL IS WHAT I HOLD..

FOR YOU ARE ME AND I AM YOU THIS LOVE
WE SHARE IS ONLY MEANT FOR TWO...
A TWO OF A KIND THAT'S NOT LEFT IN TIME...
A TWO OF A KIND WHOSE LOVE IS HELD WITH IN THE MIND...
NOW THAT WE KNOW THIS, OUR WORDS ARE OUR WITNESS THAT
KEEPS US WITH THE AMMUNITION THAT KEEP
US ON THIS MISSION OF A HAPPY LIFE...
A LIFE IN WHICH WE HAVE BEEN SEARCHING
FOR AND UNLOCKING
SO MANY HIDDEN DOORS TRAPPED IN OUR MINDS...

EASLEY SLIDING DOWN OUR SPINES ARE THESE
ELEMENTS THAT KEEP OUR HEARTS ENTWINED...

(A TRUE HEART)

BY:
LYDELL KING

A TRUE HEART WHAT DOES
THAT REALLY MEAN? SOME
ONE WHO IS LOYAL AND WILL
GIVE THEIR EVERY THING.
DOES IT MEAN TO LIE CHEAT,
OR DECEIVE OR IS IT A
MYSTERY, OR A UTILE
DISBELIEF, CAN YOU FEEL
THESE WORDS I WRITE OR
DID THEY PASS YOU BY, CAN YOU SAY YOU TRULY LOVE
ME AND LOOK INTO MY EYES? A TRUE HEART, YOU SAY I AM
YOUR LIGHT AND SHINING STAR, YET WHEN YOU ARE TRULY
NEEDED I CAN'T BE WHERE YOU ARE..
I'M ALWAYS ALONE AND SOME TIMES FEELING LOW
WOUNDING WHY MY TRUE HEART IS ALWAYS A FLAKE..
CONSTANTLY THINKING OF YOU, A MAN WITH A TRUE
HEART TO YOU, I WANT TO BE WITH YOU..

UNFINISHED WORDS

BY:
LAYCELLE KING

FIRST LOVE IS LIKE MY FIRST BORN,
WE ARE SWORN FOR EVER MORE,
YOU DON'T REALLY KNOW HOW I REALLY
FEEL. BECAUSE MY HEARTS BEEN PECKED
AT LIKE A COTTON FIELD. SO LETS REVEL
THESE THINGS THAT ARE SO REAL, SO OUR

HEARTS WON'T BE IN THE FIELDS TO BE
REVEALED LIKE GLASS STEAL.

SHARE MY WORLD

BY:
LYDELL KING

SHARE MY WORLD YOU ARE
MY WOMAN, I AM YOUR MAN,
WHAT MORE CAN I ASK FOR,
IT IS SIMPLY YOU THAT I
ADORE.
ME LOVING YOU, YOU LOVING ME,
ALWAYS AND FOREVER, I MEAN
UNTIL ETERNITY, I KNOW WE
JUST MET, YET IT SEEMS LIKE
10 YEARS, YOU ARE MY ROCK,
MY FOUNDATION, WHEN I SHED TEARS.
SHARE MY WORLD, AS I TELL YOU
ONCE AGAIN THERE IS NOTHING I
WILL KEEP FROM YOU, THERE IS
NOTHING I'LL HOLD IN, SO BE WITH
ME UNTIL THIS WORLD SHALL END
BE MY LOVE, MY WIFE, MY FRIEND,
SHARE MY WORLD.

MORE THEN YOU THINK

---◆◆◆◆◆◆---

BY:
LAYCELLE KING

LOVE IS MORE THAN JUST HEARTS AND FLOWERS AND
ROMANCE, MORE THEN CANDLE LIGHT DINNERS
AND DANCING, MORE THEN WALKS IN THE PARK
AND MOMENTS OF INTAMENT SHARING.

LOVE LAST BEYOND THOSE INITIAL STAGES. IT UNDERSTANDS
THROUGH THE DIFFICULT TIMES, CARING PAST THE
DISAGREEMENTS. IT'S LAUGHING TOGETHER WHEN THINGS
ARE GOOD, OR LAUGHING TOGETHER TO KEEP FROM CRYING
WHEN THINGS COULDN'T SEEM TO GO MORE WRONG.
IT'S PATIENCE AND COMPASSION, COMPROMISE
AND HEALING. LOVE IS FORGIVING.

(MY MIND)

BY:
LYDELL KING

THESE ARE THE THINGS THAT'S ROLLING ON
MY MIND AND AT TIMES HAVE MOST PEOPLE
BLIND AND CRYING IN SIDE FOR SOME THING
THAT'S NOT THERE.
FOR THEY ARE TO SCARED BECAUSE THEY
HAVE NEVER HAD NO BODY TH RE TO HELP
THEM GET PREPARED FOR WHAT'S REALLY OUT THERE.
NOW THAT I HAVE FOUND YOU, WE CAN
FINALLY BECOME ONE, ONE THAT WE HAVE
BEEN DESTINED TO BE. NO MORE DO WE HAVE
TO BE SCARED FOR WHAT'S OUT THERE FOR
YOU HAVE ME, ME YOUR HUSBAND TO BE,
TO DEPEND ON AS WELL AS CRY ON AND
HAVE YOUR BACK 100%

(MOM)

BY:

LAYCELLE KING

MOM I'M ASHAMED TO SAY THAT I TOOK YOU
FOR GRANTED WHEN I WAS LIVING AT HOME.
MANY TIMES IN RETURN FOR YOUR LOVE
AND AFFECTION, I PAVED YOU BACK WITH
ANGER AND UNGRATEFUL BEHAVIOR. MOM
I WAS BLIND TO YOUR SPECIAL QUALITIES,
WORSE YET, I WAS STUBBORN, UNCOMPROMISING,
SELFISH WHILE YOU WHERE ALWAYS TOLERANT,
UNDERSTANDING, COMPASSIONATE. I NOW REALIZE
JUST HOW MUCH YOU MEAN TO ME. I ONLY HOPE
AND RAY THAT YOU WILL ACCEPT MY DEEPEST
REGRETS AT MY PAST THOUGHTLESSNESS. YOU
WHERE AND NOW MORE THEN EVER, THE BEST
THING IN MY LIFE. MAY GOD BLESS YOU AND
KEEP YOU HEALTHY AND SAFE.

{BRIGHTER DAYS}

BY:

LYDELL KING

I'M LOOKING FORWARD TO SEEING MANY BRIGHTER DAYS, I KNOW SOME TIMES YOU FEEL TIME IS DELAYED, YET MAJORITY OF THE TIME WILL PASS, AS WE SIT AND THINK WHY GOD IS MAKING US WAIT, IF THIS IS REALLY TRUE LOVE LIKE WE THINK.

OUR LOVE AND MINDS WILL GROW STRONGER WHILE THE REST OF THE WORLD GETS MAJORITY WEAK. FOR FILLING OUR DREAMS AND FANTASIES, HAVING EVERY BODY AND THEIR MOMMA AMAZED TO SEE OUR BRIGHTER DAYS.

YOU COMPLETE ME, YOU MAKE ME FEEL WHOLE, YOU HAVE NO DOUBT, STOLE MY HEART AND SOUL, IT'S THOSE TWO THINGS AND MIND THAT I WANT YOU TO SAVER AND MOLD. THANK YOU LORD FOR HER HEART, MIND, BODY AND SOUL, IS WHAT I SINCERELY PRAY FOR EVERY NIGHT, IF YOU EVER WONDER IF I'M ALRIGHT OR KEEPING IT REAL, JUST PAUSE AND LISTEN TO WHAT YOUR HEART SAYS AS I BRING YOU BRIGHTER DAYS.

LETTING GO-

BY:

LAYCELLE KING

HOW DO YOU LET GO OF SOMETHING SO STRONG?

EVEN THOUGH THEY WERE THE ONE WHO DID YOU
WRONG. IT'S LIKE YOU CREATED THIS BOND
AND NOW IT'S JUST GONE.
JUST TO THINK ABOUT THE RELATIONSHIP BRINGS
TEARS TO YOUR EYES.
I WISH WE COULD START OVER WITH NO LIES.
WE BASED THE RELATIONSHIP ON FEELINGS THAT
WE THINK WE HAVE FOR ANOTHER, BUT ALL IT IS,
IS LUST TO HAVE SOME ONE TO TRUST.
YOU DON'T WANT TO BE ALONE.
SO YOU RUSH INTO SOMETHING YOU SHOULD HAVE POSTPONED.
NOW YOU ARE LEFT WITH A BROKEN HEART
AND NOWHERE TO RESTART.
YOUR LIFE IS SHATTERED WITH HATRED AND PAIN
AND MOST OF IT YOU CAN'T EXPLAIN. SO HOW DO
YOU LET GO OF SOMETHING SO STRONG? PUT YOUR
TRUST IN GOD AND HE WILL PULL YOU ALONG.

CURIOUS-

ARE YOU THINKING OF ME WONDERING WHAT AM I DOING?
IS IT NEGATIVE OR VERY POSITIVE, DO YOU TRY TO TAKE
WORDS FROM MY SOUL TO CURE YOUR BROKEN HEART, THIS
IS NOT A GAME OR SOME TYPE OF MAZE, I JUST WANT TO
KNOW HONESTLY WHERE YOU CURIOUS FROM THE START?

I DIDN'T WRITE THIS POEM TO MAKE IT RHYME, I WROTE IT TO SAY
YOU ARE ALWAYS ON MY MIND, AND I FEEL YOUR TOUCH AND
KISS ALL THE TIME. IF YOU HAVE YOUR FRONT COVERED. IT'S FOR
SURE THAT I GOT YOUR BACK, NOW TELL ME THE HONEST TRUTH,
HAVE YOU EVER WONDERED AND BEEN CURIOUS ABOUT THAT?

BY: LYDELL KING

NOTHINGS THE SAME WITHOUT YOU-

BY:

LAYCELLE KING

I SIT HERE AND STARE AT THESE 4 WALLS,
MEMORIES OF YOU ARE ALL I RECALL..
I THINK ABOUT YOU IN MY DREAMS EVERY
NIGHT JUST YOU AND ME..
I'M HOLDING YOU TIGHT WHEN WE START MAKING
LOVE LOOKING IN YOUR EYES AND KISSING YOUR
SOFT LIPS. A TEAR BEGINS TO SLOWLY DRIP.
YOU SAY I MISS YOU..
I LAY HERE ALONE EYES CLOSED IN MY BUNK,
THINKING OF YOU, I HEAR YOUR VOICE IN MY HEAD,
EVERY DAY I ASK GOD HOW MUCH MORE TIME WILL
HE KEEP US APART...
PLAYING TRICKS WITH MY MIND AND HEART.
I PACE BACK AND FORTH IN THIS CAGE THEY CALL
A CELL...
THINKING OF OUR FUTURE THAT ONLY FEW HAVE
HELD...
I WISH I COULD PUT HOW I FEEL INTO WORDS
BUT THE BEST I CAN DO IS SAY I LOVE YOU ....

!PAIN!

BY:

LYDELL KING

I HAVE ENDURED SO MUCH PAIN THROUGH OUT
DOING THIS TIME IT HAS MADE ME BETTER,
STRONGER AND SEE THE TRUE MEANING OF PAIN,
IT HAS MADE ME INTO THE MAN I AM TODAY.

FOR I CAN SEE A PERSON FOR WHO THEY ARE
AND NOT FOR WHO THEY TRY TO BE. DOING
THIS TIME HAS MADE MY MIND FREE, FOR
I CAN SEE WHY MOST PEOPLE GO THROUGH
THEIR WHOLE LIFE TRYING TO SEE AND LIVE
THEIR LIFE SO THEY CAN SEE.

FOR PAIN IS MOSTLY PHYSICAL, YET ONCE
YOU HAVE TRULLY FOUND YOURSELF, ONLY
THEN WILL YOU BE FREE.

IMMORTAL THOUGHTS

BY:

LAYCELLE KING

IMMORTAL THOUGHTS HAVE THIS BLACK MAN
HANGING FROM HIS OWN THOUGHTS.
IMMORTAL THOUGHTS HAVE ME WONDERING
WHY I EVER FOUGHT..
IMMORTAL THOUGHTS HAVE ME WANTING TO
DANCE WITH THE DEVIL WITH NO ROMANCE
BECAUSE THE DANCE WILL PROVE I'M FOREVER
HAVING IMMORTAL THOUGHTS..
AROUND AND AROUND AS MY BODY GOES THROUGH
OUT THIS CAGE MY SOUL HAS TURNED COLD.
FOR I'M FOREVER LOCKED IN THIS HELL, MORE
OF A CURSE THEN A BLESSING..
I ONCE AGAIN FIND MYSELF LOST AND SEEKING THE THINGS
IN WHICH I'VE BEEN LEAKING IMMORTAL THOUGHTS..
AS THESE 4 WALLS PUT BARS AROUND MY MIND I
INCLINE THE THINGS THAT'S LOCKED AWAY IN MY
MIND. I'M CONFINED TO IMMORTAL THOUGHTS...
I GRAB A MAC FROM MY MIND AND SHOOT IT OFF
THROUGH THESE LINES, HOPING THEY UNLOCK MANY
MINDS. INSTEAD OF LEAVING THEM BLIND AND
CONFINED TO THEIR OWN IMMORTAL THOUGHTS...

AS I FIND MYSELF-

BY:

LYDELL KING

AS I FIND MYSELF TRAPPED WITHIN THESE
FOUR WALLS I AM APPALLED FOR WHAT I SEE
AND FOR WHAT I CAN'T BE.

VICIOUS GUARDS ENVY ME BECAUSE THEY
CAN'T BE ME, AND THE COLD THING ABOUT IT
YOU SEE, I'M TRAPPED WITH IN THESE FOUR
WALLS THAT SURROUND ME.

THESE VICIOUS GUARDS FAIL TO SEE THAT
I'M A MAN, A BLACK MAN WITH A MASTER
PLAN.

AS LONG AS I HAVE THESE GUARDS ENVING
ME I WILL BE FREE MENTALLY, AND THEN AND ONLY THEN WILL
THAT BE THE POINT AND TIME WHEN THEY CAN'T BE ME CAUSE
I'M A BLACK KING THAT'S ALL SEEING AS WELL AS BEING...

FOOT STEPS

––––– ✦✦✦✦✦ –––––

BY:
LAYCELLE KING

MY FOOT STEPS ARE SMALL AND SLOW AT TIMES,
YET IT SEEMS I KEEP FOLLOWING THIS INVISIBLE
LINE OF MY FATHERS FOOT STEPS.
AT TIMES I FEEL LIKE A UTILE KIDNAPPED KID, LOST AND
CAN'T BE FOUND, YET MY FOOT STEPS KEEP GOING
ON, FOR I HAVE THIS DEEP DOWN BURNING DESIRE
TO BE LIKE SOME ONE I SO MUCH DISLIKE.
AS MY MIND FILLS UP WITH REJECTION, I STUDY FEEL BLOOD RUSH
TO MY HEAD LIKE AN ERECTION. I'M SICK OF REJECTION, I'M
TIERED OF TRYING TO MAKE THESE FUCKED UP CONNECTIONS,
WHEN THERE'S NO ONE THERE TO CONNECT WITH.
AS I LOOSE MY SENSE OF DIRECTION, I REALIZE I'VE LOST MY
CONCENTRATION, TO MY MIND, FOR MY FATHER TRYING
TO TELL ME MENTALLY TO CONTINUE TO FOLLOW HIS FOOT
LINE. MY FATHERS FOOT STEPS ARE FOREVER ETCHED ON
MY MIND, YET I'M AFRAID IT'S TIME FOR ME TO BE MY OWN
MAN AND MAKE MY OWN STEPS AND LEAVE HIS FOOT STEPS
BEHIND. WALKING THESE STEPS HAS BROUGHT ME BACK TO MY
FAILURES AND MISFORTUNES, FOR SO MANY YEARS IT SEEMS
I'VE BEEN FOREVER WALKING IN PUBBLES OF CRIED TEARS.

FOR YEARS I'VE BEEN IN FEAR THAT ONE DAY I WILL BE MY FATHERS MIRROR. AN IMAGE THAT SHELL PERISH FOR YEARS FOR IT HAS BROUGHT TO MANY TEARS, FROM THIS DAY FORWARD, I MAKE MY OWN PATH SO ONE DAY MY KIDS CAN SAY THEY FOLLOWED MY RAFT, INSTEAD OF SAYING THEY FOLLOWED MY FOOT PATH..

THE SOUL-

BY:
LYDELL KING

I LOOK OVER MY SHOULDER AND
I SEE A VISION OF ME STARING
AT ME. AS I TURN TO LOOK AT
IT HEAD ON, EYE TO EYE, I FIND
MYSELF LOOKING DEEP WITH IN
MY SOUL.
THE LIES AND ALL THE OTHER
THINGS THAT I HAVE BEEN TOLD
REAPPER, FOR IT SHOWS ME NOTHING,
YET THE TRUTH AND THE TRUE
COLORS OF OTHERS AND THEIR WORD.
I PULL MY SOUL CLOSER TO MY HEART,
AS I AM NO LONGER IN FEAR OF PAIN
FOR I HAVE MY SOUL IN TACK AND
CLOSE TO ME, EYE TO EYE WITH MY
SOUL IS THE KEY THAT HAS SET MY
MIND FREE.

<CARESSING >

+ + + + + +

BY:
LAYCELLE KING

CARESSING THIS PAGE WITH THIS PEN AND MY
HAND WISHING WE WERE IN THE SAME ROOM..
I WONDER HOW THINGS HAVE BEEN SINCE WE PARTED..
YOUR LAST TOUGH I STILL HAVE YOU FRESH IN MY MIND..
MAY BE THERE'S SOME ONE NEW WAITING AT
HOME. IS WHAT YOU TWO HAVE REALLY LOVE?
OR JUST A FACE SMILE OF FEELINGS WE ONCE SHARED..
I HOPE FOR YOU THAT HE REALLY CARES LIKE I DID AND STILL DO..
I REMEMBER LOOKING INTO YOUR EYES AND
SEEING FOREVER, HOWEVER FOREVER WAS CUT
SHORT BY MY ACTIONS AND THE COURTS.
THE LOVE I HAD FOR YOU HASN'T EVER DIMINISHED.
DON'T THINK THAT IT EVER WILL.. MY REALITY
IS SUCH A JAGGED PILL MOST AREN'T STRONG
ENOUGH TO SWOLLOW, MOST NEVER WILL HOWEVER
I HAVE AND MY THROAT IS ALMOST AS CUT UP AS MY HEART...
I GUESS THAT COMES WITH CARESSING THIS PAGE
WITH THIS PEN, AND BEING LOCKED IN..

!!ENTRAPPED MINDS!!

BY:
LYDELL KING

MY THOUGHTS SOME TIMES DRIFT,
SLOWLY AWAY, YET I MAINTAIN

MY COMPOSURE AND MANAGE
TO STAY IN THIS SUBLIMINAL

WORLD THAT WANDERS ASTRAY,
WILL I STAY HERE FOREVER OR

RETURN HOME ONE DAY? THE
MIND IS COMPLEX IN SO MANY

WAYS, AND IF NOT PUT TO USE, IT ALWAYS
DECAYS. IT'S ALSO A WEAPON, WHICH GROWS
SHARPER EACH DAY AND IN THE NIGHT, I'M
THANKFUL TO GOD AT NIGHT WHEN I PRAY..

(FRESH IN MY MIND)

BY:
LAYCELLE KING

YOU ARE FRESH IN MY MIND, AS I TAKE A
TRIP DOWN MEMORY LANE.
THE REASON WHY I TAKE THIS TRIP IS TO
LESSEN THE PAIN..
THE PAIN THAT'S SHACKLED ME DOWN FROM
HEAD TO TOE, THE PAIN THAT'S THROWN
ME IN A RAIN OF TEARS, TEARS AND

FEARS FROM NOT HAVING YOU NEAR..
SO I HOLD ON TO YOUR MEMORIES FOR

THAT'S ALL I HAVE TO HOLD ON TOO,
UNTIL THE DAY WE ARE FACE TO FACE
SO THERE'S NO CHASE, NO CHASE OF
THESE MEMORIES, NO CHASE OF THE
MIND, A CHASE THAT LEAVES PEOPLE
BLIND, WITH NO MORE FRESH MEMORIES
LEFT IN THEIR MINDS..

(7 WAYS TO THE KEY OF LOVE)

BY:

LYDELL KING

A SMILE CAN LIGHT UP A HEART.

A FROWN SETS PEOPLES WORDS APART.

A LAUGH CAN TAKE PEOPLE PLACES.

A SCREAM PUTS PAIN INTO PEOPLES FACES.

LOVE WILL MAKE YOU SMILE! BUT ONLY FOR A WHILE.

NOW ONLY TRUE LOVE AND FRIENDSHIP WILL HOLD A TRUE
WOMAN AND MAN TRUE LOVE TOGETHER FOREVER.

NOW THERE IS YOU AND ME TO BE, TO BE AS ONE FOR
EVER YOU SEE? SO NOW ARE YOU DOWN TO TAKE
THIS TRIP WITH ME TO THE WORLD OF ECSTASY?

"CHAINED TO MY OWN THOUGHTS"

BY:
LAYCELLE KING

AS I SIT IN THIS LONELY FORBIDDEN PLACE
I FIND MYSELF IN CHASE OF A THING THAT'S CALLED MY PLACE.

I WRITE THESE WORDS IN PLACE OF MY FEELINGS
THAT'S MISSED PLACED BY HATE..
I OFTEN TRY TO ESCAPE THE THINGS THAT ENTWINE MY FATE..

VOICES IN MY HEAD TELL ME I'M BEING MISLED
BY THE THINGS I DREAD THE MOST.

THE LIFE STYLE OF A CRIMINAL IS SO SUBLIMINAL ONLY
IF YOU COULD SEE IN THE MIND OF A CRIMINAL..

YOU WOULD DETECTED THE STRESS THAT
OVER WHELMS US THE BEST..
OR SOON LEADS US TO OUR DEATH. FRUSTRATION
FINALLY SETS IN AS THE WINDS BRING IN MY THOUGHTS
WHICH I WRITE DOWN WITH THIS PEN..

"COULD"

BY:

LYDELL KING

LYING ALONE IN MY CELL DON'T KNOW WHAT I'M
GONNA DO. TRYING TO FIGURE OUT IF THIS IS
IT THIS TIME, JUST CAN'T STOP THINKING ABOUT
THE WAY YOU MAKE ME FEEL INSIDE.

I JUST CAN'T GET YOU OFF MY MIND, NO MATTER HOW
HARD I TRY. COULD YOU BE THE ONE FOR ME? COULD
WE DANCE THE NIGHT AWAY? I WANNA GIVE YOU
EVERY THING, EVEN THOUGH I DON'T HAVE MUCH.

COULD YOU FALL IN LOVE WITH ME? COULD YOU
LOVE ME THE REST OF YOUR LIFE? COULD YOU
EVER BE THE ONE FOR ME THIS TIME?

I WALK AROUND IN A DAZE, THE ICE IS MELTING FROM MY
HEART. CAN I EVEN KNOW IF YOU FEEL THE SAME? ARE YOU THE
SUNSHINE THAT'S BEGGING ME TO COME IN FROM THE RAIN?

OR HAVE YOU CAME INTO MY LIFE TO TURN AROUND AND TAKE
YOUR LOVE AWAY? WHEN I LOOK INTO YOUR EYES OOH! THEY
TELL ME THAT YOUR MINE, HOWEVER I KEEP ASKING MYSELF,
COULD YOU FOREVER BE THE ONE FOR ME THIS TIME...

"RAGE"

————— ✦✦✦✦✦ —————

BY:
LAYCELLE KING

THE COURTS GAVE ME MORE TIME THEN MY
AGE..
NOW I FIND MYSELF SITTING IN THIS SIX BY
NINE CAGE..

SITTING HERE BUILDING UP MORE RAGE, AS
WALK AROUND THIS LONELY CAGE, THE PAGES
OF TIME IS STUDY TURNING IN MY MIND...
AS I STUMBLE UPON THAT FINAL CHAPTER
I AM CAPTURED IN MY OWN RAGE, FOR I'VE
BUILT MY OWN SELF CAGE IN MY MIND...
I WAS BLIND AND COULDN'T FIND MYSELF,
THAT'S WHY I HIDE FROM MYSELF. AS I WRITE
THESE WORDS, I'M LIKE A BIRD TRYING TO BE
SEEN AS WELL AS HEARD, FOR THE COURTS
ALREADY HAVE KICKED,MY LIFE TO THE CURB
LIKE A BAD ARB...

"AT LAST"

BY:
LYDELL KING

THE CHOICES, THE VOICES,
THEY GOT ME SURROUNDED,
WHICH DO I CHOOSE,
WHICH DO I LOOSE,
MY LIFE ISN'T GROUNDED,
MAKE MY CHOICES,
LET IT BE KNOWN
WHAT LIFE DO I WANT,
WHERE DO I CALL HOME?
TRUTH IS I DON'T KNOW.
CAN'T BE SO SLOW,
MAKE THE CHOICE QUICK,
ENQUIRING MINDS WANT TO KNOW,
BUT WAIT,
DON'T RUSH ME, THIS IS MY LIFE
NOT SOME NOVELTY
IN A STORE LIKE PLAY DOE.
CAN'T JUST PUT ME IN A MOLD I THINK.
I AM A BIT OF ALL MY PAST, NATIVE TO RUNAWAY
TO GANGBANGEN AND CONVICT, BACK TO NATIVE AT LAST

"ANGEL EYES"

BY:

LAYCELLE KING

ANGEL EYES ARE MY SURPRISE,
ANGELS EYES DO NOT LIE,
I LOVE YOUR ANGEL EYES...
IN THE DARK AT NIGHT YOU COME,
BRINGING LIGHT, BRINGING LOVE...
WINGS SO SOFT, GONE TO ROME..
WINGS TO GUIDE MY WAY THIS NIGHT..
HEAVENLY TO BEHOLD,
WONDROUS TO BE SHOWN...
TRIP TO WHERE IT'S BEAUTIFUL GONE TO ROME.
ALWAYS SHOWING ME SAFELY HOME.
WAITING, GUIDING, LOVING, GROWING,
AND NOW I UNDERSTAND,
ANGELS ARE ALL SEEING,
AS WELL AS ALL KNOWING, AND
YOU ARE MY ANGEL EYES..

Printed in the United States
by Baker & Taylor Publisher Services